BILLY GRAHAM
SPEAKS

Insight

from the

World's Greatest

Preacher

~ ✳ ~

BILLY GRAHAM SPEAKS

Insight

from the

World's Greatest

Preacher

JANET LOWE

John Wiley & Sons, Inc.

New York • Chichester • Weinheim • Brisbane • Singapore • Toronto

Like other *Speaks* books, *Billy Graham Speaks* was created through
the independent research of the author Janet Lowe. It has not been
authorized by its subject.

Library of Congress Cataloging-in-Publication Data:
Lowe, Janet
    Billy Graham speaks: insight from the world's greatest preacher /
by Janet Lowe.
        p.   cm.
    Includes bibliographical references.
    ISBN 0-471-34535-0 (cloth : alk. paper)

Book design and composition by Anne Scatto / PIXEL PRESS

10   9   8   7   6   5   4   3   2   1

~ * ~

*Dedicated to our daughter
Elizabeth and her family,
Charles, Edward, Tarah, Brandon,
and Vernon, a family who would
be an inspiration even to a
great preacher*

~ * ~

CONTENTS

PREFACE

If ever there was a figure who might represent the United States of America in the eyes of the world, it would be the great twentieth century evangelist Billy Graham. A towering figure physically with fair skin and light eyes, Graham even has the craggy features of the traditional image of Uncle Sam. Of course America is now more diverse than when the Uncle Sam figure was invented, but Graham symbolizes America in other ways too, with his immense energy, outspoken independence, sense of destiny, patriotism, and deep-seated religious faith.

There are many evangelists in the world, but Graham is the best known and evokes the greatest response from audiences. After one of his crusades is broadcast on television 40,000 to 50,000 letters a day pour into his Minneapolis headquarters.[1]

At the end of 1998, Graham was named the third most admired person in America. President Bill Clinton and wife Hillary were the first most admired man and woman; Pope John Paul II and Oprah Winfrey tied for second place, and Graham was named third. It was the thirty-fifth year that the evangelist was voted to the list.[2]

Graham has been with us for one-fortieth of Christian history, but when he first came on the scene in the 1940s few people in religious circles expected the brash, theatrical, young preacher to become the best-known, most widely traveled, and most sincerely influential Protestant voice of our time.

Now, nearly 60 years later, Graham has preached almost everywhere in the world, and his books are read by people of all religions. A church librarian in Anthong, Thailand, noted: "When the Buddhist priests come into our library, the favorite book they like to borrow is Billy Graham's *Peace with God*."[3]

Martin E. Marty, a professor of Christian history at the University of Chicago, says that his job is to place people in time and space. Graham's space, he says, has been global. "From an almost hard-scrabble early life in North Carolina, the precincts of small Bible colleges, and Los Angeles tent revivals, he has come to be with the Pope, one of the two best-known figures in the Christian world—or in the world, for that matter. From the years when, still in insecurity, he was a name-dropper of kings and celebrities, he has come to be the one whose name statecrafters and notables drop."[4]

Graham often is compared to the Pope, but with all due respect to the Holy Father, Graham's journey is far more surprising. Although raised a Reformed Presbyterian and associated early in his career with the

Southern Baptist denomination, Graham rose to a position of moral authority through no formal church organization.

Furthermore, Graham seldom discusses lofty, abstract, theological issues or rarely—despite an affinity for U.S. presidents and other world leaders—inserts himself into social problems and projects, except in relation to what they mean to a Christian life.

Graham made his mark by repeating over and over a simple message: That God sent his son Jesus Christ to die for our sins, and those who accept God's grace shall go to heaven and live eternally, and those who do not commit themselves to Christ are doomed to eternal separation from God, a condition known as hell.

Billy Graham is the fifth great American leader that I've written about in the *Speaks* series. Each of these subjects, the super-investor Warren Buffett, General Electric chairman Jack Welch, Microsoft Corporation founder Bill Gates, and television talk show host Oprah Winfrey, have something in common. Each of these people has forever changed the business in which they work, and they've done so by following their own instincts.

All have been intelligent and blessed with incredible energy and stamina. But more important, they all started down their career paths early; they each focused directly on their work and have not been discouraged or derailed by setbacks.

Like the others, there was little indication in Billy Graham's early life that he would achieve greatness.

He grew up in a fairly typical family for his region of the country, he attended public schools, and graduated from a quiet little midwestern college.

The most interesting revelation in writing this book has been to realize how Graham learned, grew, adapted, and expanded his abilities over the years. Born at the end of World War I, Graham grew up during the Great Depression, attended college during World War II, and began his ministerial career when newspapers, magazines, and radio were still the primary forms of mass communication. Today Graham's sermons are broadcast around the earth by satellite and the Minneapolis, Minnesota-based Billy Graham Evangelistic Association (BGEA) maintains an extensive site on the worldwide web.

His love, compassion, understanding, and patience also have grown steadily over the years. In his youth, his personality, and perhaps his soul, was a blazing, impetuous house afire. But over time the licking flames have subsided and now Graham gives off the warmth and luminescence of smouldering embers.

Although Graham may seem universally admired, that is not entirely the case. Extremely fundamental Christians, who believe that Graham is too generous in forgiving those who don't follow the Holy Bible in its strictest and most literal translation, wage relentless and sometimes frightening hate campaigns against him.

Graham has been criticized for going to communist countries or nations that are in conflict with the United States. But Graham is resolute:

"I pay no attention to them [the critics] because I'm going to preach the gospel."[5]

Despite the detractors, Graham's admirers are legion. Singer Johnny Cash, who often performed at Graham's crusades, says he has never known a greater man. Cash says the source of Graham's grandeur is his simplicity, common touch, and his childlike compassion for his fellow man.[6]

After spending time at the Graham's home in North Carolina, a *Saturday Evening Post* reporter wrote: "And the end product is made clear as we leave Montreat: it has been a busy, full morning, and yet we are completely serene. The presence of Billy Graham contains a gift of himself to others."[7]

Graham is now in his eighth decade of life and his health is poor. He suffers from Parkinson's Disease, a condition that affects the interaction between the muscles and the brain. He speaks often of impending death and the hereafter.

Writing in *Christianity Today*, Philip Yancey called upon all Christians to follow Graham's example of Christian charity. Graham, he noted, rose to prominence during an era of both political and religious narrow-mindedness:

"He was savaged for inviting Catholics onto his platform, for golfing with John Kennedy, for meeting with Jews and liberal Christians, for traveling to communist countries. Yet he met all vituperation with soft words, humility, and a gentle spirit. Eventually,

Graham's irenic spirit provided an umbrella that sheltered—and helped to mature—the entire evangelical movement. What will happen to that movement when Graham's peacemaking spirit is no longer with us?"[8]

~

Readers of *Billy Graham Speaks* should pick up the book with several thoughts in mind. The text is composed largely of Billy Graham quotations, and though every effort has been made to keep his words in context, Graham and others did not say these things in the order that they are presented. They have been organized by subject matter and in a way that allows Graham's life story to unfold. For more information on when and where a particular statement was made, please refer to the notes at the back of the book. A chronology of Graham's life and a list of his crusades have been included as well, again to help readers put Graham's words into appropriate perspective.

~

Many people made valuable contributions to this book, most specifically my husband and helper, Austin Lynas, who did a brilliant job of coordinating the extensive research that went into this project. Dr. Lon Anderson and the staff at the Billy Graham Center at Wheaton College, Wheaton, Illinois. A special thanks to Neil Sellers and Norman Sanders of the Billy Graham Training Center at The Cove near Asheville, North

Carolina. Norm Sanders gave up a Christmas vacation day to give a guided tour of the facility.

I would like to thank Myles Thompson, Jennifer Pincott, and Robin Goldstein at John Wiley & Sons for their hard work and dedication. Alice Fried Martell, my literary representative, as always, has been loyal and supportive. I am forever grateful to Jolene Crowley, Phyllis Kenney, Elizabeth Husmann, and many others who gave their opinions and lent balance to this work.

~

Each book in the *Speaks* series has been a joy to compile because it presents the opportunity to examine in depth, the life and philosophy of a remarkable human being. The objectivity, wisdom, humor, and soaring spirits of people like Billy Graham never ceases to impress. Whether or not you can agree with Graham's beliefs about religion and spirituality, you most likely will be moved by the man himself.

I hope you enjoy reading this book as much as I have enjoyed preparing it.

Janet Lowe
Del Mar, California
JANUARY, 1999

Billy Graham Speaks

Insight

from the

World's Greatest

Preacher

~ ✻ ~

MAKING OF AN EVANGELIST

BILLY SUNDAY

When Billy Graham was a child, his parents took him to Charlotte to hear America's most famous and flamboyant evangelist, Billy Sunday.

> *"I was about four years old and too young to understand that my namesake had preached to the largest crowds in the history of his time. I did know that he was a former baseball player and sometimes started his service by running across the platform and sliding up to the pulpit on his stomach, as you'd steal home base in a ball game. I was held silent by the promise that if I squirmed, Billy Sunday would personally run me out of his tabernacle. No threat was necessary, however. The tension in the huge throng and the dynamic gestures of the athletic evangelist held me spellbound for the entire two hour service."[1]*

～

Born in 1862, Sunday played for the Chicago White Stockings baseball team from 1883 to 1891. An avid fundamentalist, he denounced science, liquor, and political liberalism.

An Atlanta newspaper ran this description of a Billy Sunday crusade:

"When Sunday came to Atlanta in 1917, he preached three sermons on the first day to congregations totaling 30,000. The revival was held in a temporary tabernacle at Jackson and Irwin Streets Northeast. At a climactic point in a sermon, Sunday would grab a chair, leap up and then, with one foot on the chair and the other on the pulpit, implore sinners to repent and God to forgive. 'So it went for seven weeks,' wrote historian Franklin Garrett. 'It was one of Atlanta's great emotional experiences.'"[2]

In his colorful way, Sunday had an answer for everything:

"Going to church," said Sunday, "doesn't make you a Christian any more than going to a garage makes you an automobile."

To those who said revival meeting Christianity soon wears off, Sunday replied, "They tell me a revival is only temporary, so is a bath, but it does you good."[3]

Sunday was part of an American tradition of traveling religious orators, who with passion and idealism, influenced America since its earliest colonial days. It was this heritage that Billy Graham would become part of.

~

FARMING, GIRLS, AND BASEBALL

"I lived on a farm in North Carolina where I was the oldest son in a devout Presbyterian family. Each morning I was required to milk 10 to 20 cows before breakfast, and I had to attend every worship service conducted at the Presbyterian church to which my parents belonged. I secretly rebelled against both."[4]

~

As a youngster, Billy Graham could not imagine that he would lead a religious life:

"Sometimes parents can try to force religion down their children and make them sick. I'm not sure that my parents gave me too much, but I do know I went to church only to please them and to school mainly to play baseball."[5]

~

"When I was young, I wasn't sure what I was going to be. I knew that I didn't want to be an undertaker. And I knew that I certainly didn't want to be a clergyman. I had sat through too many dry sermons, I suppose." [6]

~

Charlotte, North Carolina, surely noticed young Billy. As a teen he was full of rebellion against his religious upbringing. Perhaps he wasn't wild by today's standards, but he was scrappy, noisy, and an aggressive driver.

3

"My life had little purpose, but I remember making myself one promise: I would never become an undertaker or a preacher. I could see no point in going to school at all. 'What does a farmer need to know about English or science?' I asked myself."[7]

~

"I loved, I hated, I walked on clouds. I groveled in despair. I had all the youthful hang-ups. My world at times seemed to be falling apart. The Great Depression of the thirties was on. Hitler was on the march across Europe. Manchuria had been invaded. . . . understood little and resented my parents, my teachers, my humdrum life as a farmhand and high-school student. There has always been a gap between generations—there always will be. I rather expect it was meant to be."[8]

~

Graham's sister, Catherine, recalls, "He was in love with a different girl every day. He really did like the girls. And they liked him."[9]

~

Graham acknowledges having a good time with the girls, sometimes kissing until his lips were chapped, but says: "I never went any further. I never touched another woman until I was married, in any way beyond kissing."[10]

~

4

But from the beginning Billy stood out. His mother once said of him: "Billy just isn't normal. He's got too much energy."[11]

FOUNDATIONS OF FAITH IN THE FAMILY

Both of Billy Graham's grandfathers, Crook Graham and Ben Coffey, descendants of Scottish Calvinist immigrants, fought for the Confederacy in the Civil War and were wounded.

When he came home from the war with a bullet in his shank, Crook Graham had a powerful hankering for raw, white whiskey. He spent most of his life haphazardly running his farm, drinking, or recovering from a hangover. In the meantime, he fathered 11 children, including Franklin, Billy's father. One family member noted that "What Frank did most while his daddy was still alive was just sort of generally stay out of his way."[12]

~

Ben Coffey, less one eye and one leg, married and had a number of daughters. One of those daughters carried the name of the son he wanted, Morrow.

~

Dairy farmer Franklin Graham courted Morrow Coffey for six years. When the bride and groom left on their five-day honeymoon, Morrow carefully tucked a Bible into her suitcase, "I just wouldn't have felt like a clean person without my Bible with me."[13]

Two years, later on November 7, 1918, Billy Franklin Graham was born. Billy would revere and love his mother all of her life.

～

"Yeah," said Billy's brother Melvin, "Billy was always the sweet one with Mother, but she used to whip me about every time she was awake." Yet Melvin and Billy were close. In 1975 Melvin was to undergo brain surgery. Before he was taken into the operating room, Billy leaned over him and said, his eyes dampening, "Melvin—I just want you to know. I love you."

Melvin later said of Billy: "I think he's just the finest man I've ever known of. He's always been perfect to me. In fact I think he's bent over backward to make sure that I didn't feel left aside—like whenever I go somewhere he is, he'll introduce me to everybody, and make sure I have the best place to sit."[14]

～

Billy's relationship to his father was always prickly, though. Franklin Graham, called Frank, was described thus by an acquaintance: "there just wasn't a whole lot of levity in him. He was a tight old Scotsman, actually, dry and proper as a persimmon."[15]

～

Grady Wilson, who later became one of Billy's closest associates, noted, "Mr. Graham's word was his bond, but he was awful astute too. He was right astute, for instance, on that water-line business—he somehow managed to persuade the city to run a water line out to his place, and then he turned around and charged everybody along it about a hundred dollars to tap in."[16]

~

Yet Frank Graham's education was limited:

> *"My father never knew much about geography. When I decided to go to Korea to spend Christmas with the troops, he asked me where Korea was."[17]*

~

Though they always were Christians, it wasn't until Graham's parents lost all their savings in the bank failures of the Great Depression that religion became central to their lives. Before that, according to a friend, "He [Frank] and Morrow were just nominal church-goers, but after that bank thing, they began holding Bible meetings in their house; that's when they really began to lay hold of deeper spiritual truths."[18]

~

Frank Graham continuously worried about the state of his own soul, said Billy: "I can remember at church or Christian businessmen's meetings when he was called on to lead in prayer, he would stand up there praying and the tears would start coming down his cheeks."[19]

Franklin apparently felt that he himself actually had been meant to preach, or to serve some Christian calling. Then, when his son Billy began to achieve celebrity as an evangelist, Frank proclaimed, "My mind has been made clear on a matter which has bothered me for 45 years. Now I feel I have the answer. The Lord had other plans for me—he put me out to plowing corn and milking cows, because my part was to raise a son who, in due time, would preach the gospel all over the world."[20]

Late in Frank Graham's life, Melvin recalls, "when he was home he always thought he was at Billy's. He'd suddenly look around and say, 'Well, well, Billy's got a house just like ours. How about that. How did he get a house just like ours?' He seemed real pleased. After sitting there awhile and looking around and marveling over this, he'd say, 'Well now, it's getting too late to stay here any longer, I got to get on back home now.'" Melvin would take his father outside, help him into the car, drive him around a few blocks, and then take him back to the house. Frank would mumble happily as they pulled back up the driveway, "Now. Now. Awful nice being over at Billy's, but this is more like it now. . . ."[21]

Graham and his father were of different generations, and at times seemed to live in different worlds. When

Frank died and the family were all at the funeral home, Billy turned to his sister and said, "I wish I could cry. I wish I could, but I can't."[22]

BILLY'S CONVERSION

When Billy Graham was 16 years old, a famous preacher named Mordecai Ham conducted an evangelistic campaign in Charlotte.

Descended from eight generations of Baptist preachers, Ham knew from childhood what he was meant to do.

"From the time I was eight years old," Ham explained, "I never thought of myself as anything but a Christian. At nine I had definite convictions that the Lord wanted me to preach."[23]

The plain-spoken Ham aimed his admonitions directly at the people he believed to be sinners, especially those who drank, manufactured, or sold alcohol. He was a relentless supporter of Prohibition and many of his crusades were directed at whiskey moonshiners. The moonshiners often tried to disrupt his crusades, and sometimes became violent, but Ham was undeterred.

∼

Mordecai Ham's first words at his November 1934 fall crusade in Charlotte were: "There's a great sinner in this place tonight."

Billy thought, "Mother's been telling him about me."[24]

More than 2,000 people attended Ham's service, a larger crowd than Graham had ever seen. The young man listened, spellbound:

> *"The fascination of an old-fashioned revival is hard to explain to anybody who never experienced one.... As I listened, I began to have thoughts I had never known before. Something began to speak to my heart. On the way home I was quiet and thoughtful. Next night, all my father's mules and horses could not have kept me away from the meeting."*[25]

That next night Graham did not respond to the altar call, and in an attempt to avoid Ham's pointed finger, he joined the choir. By sitting behind Ham, Graham thought the evangelist's magnetism might not be as strong.

∼

Graham's move to the choir proved futile. The choir sang "Just as I am," then switched to "Almost Persuaded." The soulful hymns worked their magic and Billy could no longer resist Ham's altar call.

> *"I remember that I felt very little emotion. I had a deep sense of peace and joy, but I shed no tears and I was not at all certain what was happening. In fact when I saw that others had tears in their eyes, I felt like a hypocrite, and this disturbed me."*[26]

∼

> *"That simple repentance and open commitment to Jesus Christ changed my life."*[27]

~

Graham says that his conversion was part of a complex internal process:

"I willed to seek Christ . . . it was partly intellect, partly emotion, but primarily will."[28]

~

From then on Billy Graham went to hear evangelists whenever they came to town and became friends with the preacher Jimmie Johnson. One day when Johnson was sermonizing to some prisoners in a jail, he turned to Graham and said, "Here's a young man who can tell you what it's like to be converted."

Graham's first attempt at public speaking was not easy for him:

"Somehow I got to my feet and said that being born again gave you a new and different life, that even the trees and the flowers looked different. Three or four sentences were all I could manage, but a great thrill filled me."[29]

~

Soon after Graham graduated from high school, the shy young man got work as a door-to-door Fuller Brush salesman. It sounded like an easy job, but it was the Depression and people were too poor to buy a luxury like a new brush. One woman was so angered by door-to-door salesmen that she dumped a pitcher of water on Graham from an upstairs window. "Get your blankety-blank hide off my property," she said.[30]

Graham worked all summer and, despite the difficulties, proved himself a natural salesman. He had the highest sales of anyone in his group.

PREACHING ON THE STREET

After a trying but successful summer peddling Fuller brushes, Graham decided to go to college rather than follow his father into farming. His friend, the evangelist Jimmie Johnson, recommended his alma mater, Bob Jones University, then based in Cleveland, Tennessee. Graham enrolled but never did fit in at the privately owned fundamentalist Christian school, which since has moved to Greenville, South Carolina. Bob Jones U. is known for its curfews, modest dress codes, and chaperoned dating parlors. When Graham went there it was a racially segregated school, and even today Bob Jones U. maintains a strict antigay and lesbian policy.[31]

The discipline was crippling to the out-going, charismatic Graham, who was accustomed to a relatively free-wheeling life. Furthermore, Graham's high school had not prepared him well enough for college math and science and his grades were poor.

"He was a totally liberated personality," said Jimmie Johnson. "I mean, he would just do the most unexpected, fascinating things—like once, when he was driving us all back from Charleston, the sun visor kept falling down in front of him, and finally he just reached up and snatched it right off and threw it out the window. Those kinds of little things."[32]

Billy decided to leave the school and told Dr. Bob Jones of his choice. Jones was not happy with this turn of events because he thought Graham had the voice to become a preacher. Jones told him: "If you're a misfit at Bob Jones College, you'll be a misfit anywhere."[33]

~

A roommate of Graham's at Bob Jones had gone on to the Florida Bible Institute and suggested the school. Shortly after Billy arrived at the institute, the founder, Dr. W. T. Watson, gathered everyone together and announced that the Bible Institute was in financial trouble and asked everyone to pray for God's help.

> *"That evening a telegram arrived from a man who said he had felt strangely burdened to send a check for $10,000 to Dr. Watson. That experience, coming when I was just beginning the Christian life, strengthened my prayer life and deepened my sense of the reality of God."[34]*

~

One Saturday night, a visiting minister asked Graham to preach the next morning at the Baptist church in Bostwick. Graham tried to get out of the assignment, saying he didn't know how to preach.

"I'll do my best," said Graham, who earlier had secretly prepared four sermon outlines. Graham studied and prayed all that night. Billy remembers that first sermon:

"As I began my knees shook and my hands and brow became wet. I raced through my first sermon outline, then the second, then the third. At the end of eight minutes I had been through all four sermons. I sat down. Nobody ever failed more ignominiously. The experience convinced me I was not called to preach."[35]

~

Graham felt that his poor performance was a sign that God had something else in mind for him:

"If God wanted me, I told myself, I should clearly hear his call. Let me explain about being 'called.' It is my view that whoever serves God in the pulpit of a church should be called of God. Like conversion, it comes to a person in various ways. If God summons, you know it, you feel it, and you cannot do other than obey it. . . . I remember feeling that, despite all arguments to the contrary, God did want me to preach."[36]

~

Billy made his final decision to become a minister at midnight on the 18th green of a golf course:

"One night, on the Temple Terrace Golf Course outside Tampa, Florida, where I was attending school, God spoke to my heart. It was about midnight. The full moon was up. It looked beautiful through the palm trees on the Hillsborough River. God had been speaking to me for several days, for several weeks. I

got to my knees, and with tears coming down my cheeks, I said, 'O God, I'll go where you want me to go. I'll be what you want me to be.' And from that moment on I have sensed the leading and the direction of God in my life."[37]

~

For two years Graham—who was six feet two inches tall and extremely thin—practiced his craft, preaching outdoors to the birds and alligators, in front of bars and taverns, and at the Tampa City Mission. "One saloon keeper tossed me out right into a ditch," Graham recalls with pride.[38]

~

"At long last, I knew where I was going and what God wanted me to do."[39]

~

Very soon, congregations began to hear of Graham's energetic high-powered style and asked him to preach in their churches. Little by little, he learned to deal with an audience and to direct his message.

"In my early sermons, I placed too much emphasis on judgment and hell. I didn't temper my message with love as much as I should have, and I didn't relate it sufficiently to social concerns and everyday life. Possibly I also didn't explain theological points adequately, because I was confused myself. This was a matter of simply not knowing. On the whole, I must say that my sermons were quite inadequate."[40]

~

Graham soon learned the importance of thinking before speaking when Jimmie Johnson asked Graham to tell prison inmates about his conversion. Billy began with the inappropriate greeting: "I'm so glad to see so many of you out this afternoon."[41]

~

In the summer after his junior year, the pastor of the big Tampa Gospel Tabernacle, Dean Minder, asked Graham to take over preaching duties for six weeks.

As Graham practiced his sermons on Saturdays in the tabernacle, the janitor sometimes listened and gave him useful pointers. Later, in 1939, Graham was preaching at the Peniel Baptist Church, south of Palatka, Florida, when the pastor asked him what Baptist church he belonged to.

The pastor was stunned to learn that Graham was a Presbyterian. The Baptist congregation would not accept that, he said.

The next Sunday the pastor, the Reverend Cecil Underwood, and the Peniel congregation immersed Graham in the waters of Silver Lake. Graham was ordained a Baptist minister later that summer.[42]

~

As Graham was finishing up at the Florida Bible Institute, family friends offered to provide a year's tuition at Wheaton College, a religious school, in Illinois. Some of Billy's friends advised him not to go, that he had enough education. Graham knew, however, that he was not fully prepared for a career in the ministry. After much soul searching, he decided to take the offer:

> *"When I made up my mind I called home. Today my mother sometimes talks about that call. 'Billy thinks he made up his own mind, but I tell you, that boy was prayed into Wheaton.'"*[43]

THE LORD PROVIDES A PARTNER

"Billy, have you ever in all your life known one single real Christian who lives a Christian life 24 hours of every day?" a skeptic once asked Graham. He replied, "Yes, my wife."[44]

∼

Graham first met his wife, Ruth McCue Bell, when a friend introduced them: "Billy, this is the girl I was telling you about."

> *"I turned around and saw a beautiful, hazel-eyed, slender girl of 19, who was already a junior [at Wheaton College]. I was so flustered and embarrassed I knew I made no sense in my greeting. It was love at first sight."*[45]

∼

Ruth is the daughter of Dr. Nelson Bell, who, at the time of Ruth's birth, served as a medical missionary in a village some 300 miles north of Shanghai. Ruth was born and raised in China and attended school in Pyongyang, North Korea.

~

When Billy and Ruth Graham made a 16 day, 2,000-mile journey through eastern China in 1988, she said: "I always looked on China as home. There is a strange magnetic pull and there is this old longing to go back home."[46]

~

Graham dated the independent Ruth for many months, when she would let him, and he waited months more for her answer to his proposal. In July 1941 she sent him a letter to Florida where he was preaching. It said, "I'll marry you." When he read it, Graham took off and ran until he was exhausted. When he got to his room he read and reread the letter. That evening he stepped up to the pulpit and preached. When he was done, the pastor turned and whispered to him, "Do you know what you said?" Graham answered, "No."

"Neither do the people," said the pastor.

Shortly afterward Graham used a "love offering" of $165 from a church in Charlotte to buy an engagement ring.

"A diamond big enough to be seen with a magnifying glass!"

Ruth wired her parents, "Bill has offered me a ring. Shall I wear it?" Her parents wired back, "Yes, if it fits."[47]

~

For a while before they were married, Ruth lived near a sanatarium where her sister Rosa was ill with tuberculosis. During the long days and nights spent helping nurse her sister, she had the opportunity to think about her life and her desire to serve as a missionary in Tibet. Doubts crept in about her engagement to Graham. She wrote him a letter, telling him that she did not think she was in love with him and that they probably should not get married. When she returned to Wheaton, Billy asked if she wanted to give the ring back. No, she said, but Ruth explained that she really was meant to be a missionary.

"Listen," he said, "do you or do you not think the Lord has brought us together?"

"Yes," Ruth confessed.

"Then," he said firmly, "I'll do the leading and you'll do the following."

Ruth later remarked with a twinkle in her eye, "I've been following him ever since."[48]

~

Ruth said she sensed that Billy "knew God in a very unusual way." In her own prayers she said, "Lord, if you let me serve you with that man, I'd consider it the greatest privilege in my life."[49]

Graham says, "Ruth was the one who had the greatest influence in urging me to be an evangelist."

Puzzled, Ruth replied, "I thought *God* called you."

Graham responds, "Well, he told me through you too."[50]

~

"She seemed to me like the answer to King Solomon's question, and mine: 'A wife of noble character, who can find? She is worth far more than rubies.'"[51]

~

Ruth conceded that as he grew more mature her husband became better looking than he was when they were first married. She described him then as a beanpole.

"There was a seriousness about him," Ruth added, "there was a depth. He was much older in every way than the other students on the campus. He was a mature man, he was a man who knew God; he was a man who had a purpose, a dedication in life; he knew where he was going."[52]

~

Ruth may well have been Billy's dream girl, but in his eyes, she still needed a little improvement. Graham, who followed a strict exercise regimen of wrestling, jogging, and calisthenics, did not approve of Ruth's health habits, which precluded getting out of breath for anything. He started work on her during their engagement.

Ruth wrote, "Saturday night, he presented me with

a bag of grapefruit and oranges and a box of vitamin pills . . . and the order to go upstairs and clothe myself warmly. Then he marched me up to the end of Howard Street, where houses are nil and he started in. Sixty times he made me jump, feet apart and clap my hands over my head and 60 times he made me hold my arms out and touch first right hand to left foot, and then left hand to right foot. There was no pleading for mercy and no teasing him out of the notion."

Graham's lectures on the merits of good diet, sufficient sleep and exercise apparently "went in one ear and out the other."[53]

~

Graham had great difficulty with long absences from his wife. On a Scottish Crusade in 1955 he wrote in one of the many letters to her: "You have no idea how lonesome it is without you! In thinking about my message tonight, I'd give anything if you were here to talk it over with."

Graham's despair must have been apparent to his team. His associate, Lee Fisher, wrote to Ruth, "Hurry on over, Bill's about to languish away. He tries to act like he's self-sufficient, but he's a perfect fool about your coming."[54]

~

Ruth Graham was philosophical about the long separations from her husband. "I'd rather have a little of Bill than a lot of any other man," she said.[55]

~

Yet homecomings were special, recalled daughter Gigi (Virginia): "Every time they got back together, it was like a honeymoon. They shared a lot of physical love. That was very reassuring for me."[56]

~

Ruth Graham apparently had a traditional view of her role: "The finest statesmen, authors, painters, musicians, businessmen, doctors and scientists have all been men. There are two areas in which women are best—as wives and mothers. We have our field and our role to play, so why compete with men? I have found my niche. I know what God has intended for me and I am happy and content in it."[57]

~

Nevertheless, all three of Billy's and Ruth's daughters have had active careers—teaching, preaching, and writing about their faith, while at the same time caring for families.

Gigi wrote in her book *Passing It On*: "Mother always taught me . . . 'There are times to quit submitting and start outwitting.'"[58]

~

Graham says: "I'll lie there, and you know how well read Ruth is, she seems to know everything about everything, and I'll lie there and kid her, 'One thing about you, you're just so unread, you're just so out of it.' . . . It's wonderful now just to lie there in bed, the two of us, and hold each other and talk."[59]

～

Ever since he became a preacher, Graham has traveled. Early in his career he was invited to preach at the Elyria, Ohio, First Baptist Church. Ruth was home, ill in the hospital. Billy had $21, a twenty and a single, in his pocket. After the collection was taken, the usher, in a surprising move, handed the collection tray to the host pastor and to Graham.

> *"I reached into my pocket for the dollar, dropped it into the plate. Suddenly I saw that it was the $20 bill. My heart sank. I now admit it was not a very cheerful gift."*[60]

At the end of his visit the churchmen handed Billy a train ticket to Chicago and a check for $95.

Later he reported to Ruth how generous he'd been, but she set him straight, saying that since he'd given the $20 bill by mistake, he couldn't be all that saintly in God's eyes.

～

But the Grahams also had problems that other couples face. Ruth sometimes had difficulty penetrating Billy's chronic preoccupation with his work. One day she was planning a meal for guests who were coming to dinner; she asked Billy, "What would you like to have on the menu?"

23

Billy replied: "Uh-huh."

Ruth then rattled off, "I thought we'd start off with tadpole soup."

"Uh-huh."

"And then there is some lovely poison ivy growing in the next cove which would make a delightful salad."

"Uh-huh."

"For the main dish, I could try roasting some of those wharf rats we've been seeing around the smokehouse lately, and serve them with boiled crabgrass and baked birdseed."

"Uh-huh."

"And for dessert we could have a mud souffle and ..." Her voice trailed off as he stirred.

"What were you saying about wharf rats?"[61]

◦

Ruth Graham has written several books of her own. In her book *Legacy of a Pack Rat*, she was quite frank about her own habits and those of her husband.

> *"She has some stories about me that I'd just as soon she left out."*[62]

◦

The Grahams raised 5 children and now have 22 grandchildren. As they've grown older, the Grahams have grown closer.

Graham and Ruth kissed good-bye in West Germany, as she headed to Asia to deliver a speech and he headed home to North Carolina for a short stay before another crusade.

"You know, when my wife left me yesterday, I broke down and cried. I just couldn't bear to think of being three or four weeks without her. That represents a real change in our lives. Up until a few years ago we were so used to coming and going that we didn't think much about it. But now all five of our children are on their own, so there are only the two of us, and we have become very dependent on each other. Ruth contributes to me emotionally and intellectually, and I do to her, in ways I never dreamed two people of our age would rely on each other."[63]

～

Billy Graham talks further about his marriage:

"I believe that as Ruth and I walk, day by day, in fellowship with God, there's a happiness that the average person doesn't understand. It's just for those who know God. I think that's true even in the sex experience with my wife. I'm practically impotent now because of the problems that I face, but it goes beyond the experience of people that are just out for . . . it's the commitment of love. Agape . . . it's a deeper love than Eros love. It's the love that only God gives. If two people who have that are making love, there's something to it that has a deeper dimension than Eros love."[64]

～

~ ✳ ~

DR. BELL

Perhaps because Graham and his own father led such different lives, Billy became very close to Ruth's father, Dr. Nelson Bell:

> *"My own father was a dairy farmer, so on many major issues I went to my father-in-law, because he was a churchman and a missionary and knew the church situation."*[65]

~

Dr. Bell, Ruth, and the rest of the Bells, who were devout Presbyterians, had an enormous influence on Billy's growth and development as an evangelist. For example, they persuaded Billy away from his unspoken conviction "that a vigorous scriptural faith could not dwell within the great denominations."[66]

~

Dr. Bell, a well-respected surgeon and religious leader, had an outlook well to the right of Graham on the issue of communism and racial issues. He reportedly was uncomfortable with the civil rights movement of the 1960s, and felt that it disrupted social discipline and order. Someone who heard him speak on a number of occasions remarked: "Dr. Bell was one of those minds who could make prejudice perfectly plausible."[67]

~

Yet, Dr. Bell seemed to believe in his son-in-law's mission: "Billy has a keen sense of destiny."[68]

~

After Dr. Bell's death in 1973, Graham's sister Jean said of her brother: "I think Billy Frank began turning more and more to Ruth to sort of take her daddy's place. He began to depend on her for that kind of strength he used to get from Dr. Bell."[69]

~ ✳ ~

A HOME IN MONTREAT

Billy and Ruth settled near her parents when their family was young and he was frequently on the road. Montreat, North Carolina, is a tiny town, and at the time was populated mainly by retired missionaries.

Their first home was small and near a busy road. The Grahams were looking for a piece of property on which to build a new quieter home but they were tight for money. However, they were offered some land in a 150-acre hollow in the Blue Ridge Mountains above Montreat, a few miles from where they lived. They went up to inspect the property. Ruth loved it and Graham said, "I leave it up to you to decide."

Then Billy left on another preaching mission. Ruth borrowed money from the bank and bought the cove while he was gone.

When he returned, he was astounded when she told him the deal was done. "You *what?*" he gasped.[70]

~

When Graham came home from a crusade to India in 1956, he found his new mountainside retreat finished and awaiting him. To fulfill her dream of a rustic log house, Ruth bought and disassembled old log cabins from all over the area. Some of the money from Graham's first book, *Peace with God*, was used to build the house.[71]

~

As the years passed and Graham's fame spread, the secluded getaway, which Ruth named Little Piney Cove, became increasingly important to his well-being:

"My greatest longing is for privacy."[72]

~

Despite its comfort, the Graham home is not imposing. The world champion boxer Muhammad Ali visited Graham at home and observed, "I thought he'd live on a thousand-acre farm and we drove up to this house made of logs. No mansion with crystal chandeliers and gold carpets, but the kind of a house a man of God would live in. I look up to him."[73]

LEARNING TO PREACH YEAR BY YEAR

Billy Graham's first pulpit call was to the Western Springs Baptist Church, in Western Springs, Illinois. The animated young preacher soon was broadcasting a radio show and helped start the Youth for Christ movement aimed at junior high and high school students. And although he accepted the post only reluctantly upon the death of its respected dean, Graham became president of Northwestern Schools, a liberal arts college, Bible school, and theological seminary in Minneapolis, Minnesota. Through it all, he continued to develop the evangelistic art.

As Billy's evangelism began to catch on, Ruth told him when he was preaching "too loud, too fast." Once she told him he "pranced around like an uppity pig" in the pulpit. "Bill, Jesus . . . just preached the gospel, and that's all he has called you to do!"[74]

∼

Graham later recalled his preaching of the early 1940s:

"I had a lapel microphone and I'd walk back and forth and preach as though there was no amplification . . . back then I preached with much more fire and vigor. Part of that was youthfulness, part of it was intensity, part of it was conviction. And part of it was . . . part of it was ignorance. I've traveled now to 85 countries and I've become friends with people in different parts of the world and seen how they live. I think I'm definitely more tolerant than I was back then."[75]

∼

His determination to learn to be a better preacher paid off. When he is at the pulpit, Graham's focus on the task is absolute. *The Saturday Evening Post* wrote of Graham: "His concentration is such a major part of his intellectual capacities that you can almost feel it."[76]

BILLY CONVERTS A MOBSTER AND IS DISCOVERED BY A NATION

Billy Graham had been preaching for six years, but his first major crusade was in Los Angeles in 1949. A great "canvas cathedral," the largest tent ever built at the time, was set up at Washington and Hill streets in downtown L.A. A huge sign hung from the tent proclaiming "Things are happening . . ." Indeed Graham drew a crowd. An average of 6,500 people were seated in the tent for every service, with another 1,000 or so gathered outside. Over the two months of the crusade, it is estimated that 350,000 people came to hear the amazing new evangelist speak.[77]

~

A youthful Billy Graham, with dark, wavy hair rising above blazing, deep set eyes, thundered, pointed his finger, shook his fist, and electrified the city. He drilled home the message that Los Angeles was "a city of wickedness and sin" and warned that the only choices before its citizens were revival or judgment. As was becoming the style of the Graham crusades, Graham's potent presentation was followed by the words of an old American hymn, "softly and tenderly Jesus is calling, come home."[78]

Graham's sermons included one that centered on

the recent announcement by President Harry Truman that the Soviet Union had just exploded an atomic weapon. Graham shouted:

"Across Europe at this very hour there is stark, naked fear among the people . . . An arms race, unprecedented in the history of the world, is driving us madly towards destruction!"

Another sermon was particularly uncomplimentary to Los Angeles, clearly referring to the charge that communists had penetrated the film industry:

"Western culture and its fruits had its foundations in the Bible, the Word of God, and in the revivals of the Seventeenth and Eighteenth Centuries. Communism, on the other hand, had decided against God, against Christ, against the Bible, and against all religion. Communism is not only an economic interpretation of life—Communism is a religion that is inspired, directed, and motivated by the Devil himself who has declared war against almighty God. . . . the Fifth Columnists, called Communists, are more rampant in Los Angeles than any other city in America. . . . in this moment I can see the judgment hand of God over Los Angeles. I can see judgment about to fall."[79]

∽

The week the Los Angeles crusade was slated to end, Graham arrived at the tent one evening to find reporters and photographers everywhere. He pulled one of the reporters aside and asked about the sudden interest. He was told it was started by a memo sent down from newspaper publisher William Randolph Hearst that said "puff Graham." Apparently Hearst was impressed with what he heard when he and his paramour, Marion Davies, had dressed in disguise and slipped in to hear Graham speak.

The blaze of nationwide publicity drew huge crowds in the following nights and Graham decided to extend the crusade one week after another. He was a sudden celebrity, eventually finding himself on the cover of *Time*, *Newsweek*, and *Life* magazines, and being covered by all the wire services.

The story spread quickly around Los Angeles on November 7 that Graham had converted Jim Vaus, a notorious gangster wiretapper and minion of crime kingpin Mickey Cohen. Rumors were rampant that Cohen would have Vaus rubbed out.

Vaus pleaded with the evangelist to speak on his behalf to his boss. Graham said he would talk to anybody about Jesus Christ. One evening Vaus and Graham secretly slipped away to meet the mobster. Mickey Cohen was friendly but a little awed at meeting a famous evangelist. He asked Graham what he would like to drink. Graham asked for a Coca-Cola, and Cohen said, "That's fine. I'll have one too."

Vaus then told Cohen that he'd come forward at Graham's tent meeting to accept Jesus Christ as his saviour and what joy it had brought to him.

Graham explained the gospel as simply as he could, praying for the right words. Cohen said that though he was of a different religion, he wished Vaus well.

After a brief prayer, Graham and Vaus slipped out, taking care not to be seen. The next day, however, the visit to Mickey Cohen was plastered all over the papers.

"To this day, I have not found out how the press knew we were there. I continued my prayers for Mickey, with the hope that he would trust Christ. I have since seen Mickey a number of times. He is now in prison, and I still pray for his conversion."[80]

J. Arthur Vaus later became a social worker in Harlem, New York, and often gave testimonies at Graham revivals, called "From Crime to Christ."

∽

Henry Luce, the founder of *Time* and *Life* magazines, went to one of Graham's crusades and also was impressed. He later became a friend of Graham's. Billy apparently complained to Luce that *Time* magazine had sent a "secularist, ignorant and suspicious of the concept and message of evangelism" reporter to cover the Los Angeles crusade in 1949.

"Would you send a dress designer to cover a ball game?" Graham asked Luce.

"He [Luce] and I became very close friends," says Graham. "*Time* . . . pushed me all the time by carrying everything I did, almost." Over time more stories appeared in the media about Graham than about almost any U.S. president.

"Let's see, I was on the front cover of Look *at least seven or eight times, on the front cover of* Newsweek *seven or eight times, and on the front cover of* Life *four times."*[81]

~

The attention Graham received after the first Los Angeles crusade astounded him:

"To me it was like a bolt of lightning out of a clear sky. I was bewildered, challenged, and humbled by the sudden avalanche of opportunities that deluged me. I was bewildered because I had no formal theological training. I had never been to seminary; in college I had majored in anthropology."[82]

BILLY GRAHAM'S VISION OF CHRISTIANITY

FAITH

"Over the years, I have been asked how I can be sure that God speaks. And I must reply that this is not a matter of words or ideas or the ordinary processes of perception. Instead, it is often subjective, and is a powerful and wonderful certainty. How do you know you're in love? A mother knows, a sweetheart knows. How do I know God's will . . . I know."[1]

During an interview, British television host David Frost asked Billy Graham: "How do you know you're not wrong [about your message of faith]?" Graham replied:

"Because I've had a personal experience with Christ. Because my faith is grounded in a relationship with God that has proved in the laboratory of personal experience through these years."[2]

GOD

"God is a Spirit, Infinite, Eternal, and Unchangeable."[3]

~

"Who is God? What is He like? How can we be sure He exists? When did He begin? Can we know Him? . . . we are daily faced with the miracle of life and the mystery of death, of the glory of flowering trees, the magnificence of the star-filled sky, the magnitude of mountains and of sea. Who made all this? Who conceived the law of gravity by which everything is held in its proper place? Who ordered the day and the night and the regular procession of the seasons?

"The only possible answer is that all these things and many more are the work of a supreme creator. As a watch must have a designer, so our precision-like universe has a great designer. We call him God."[4]

~

"The Bible declares God to be spirit *. . . what do you think of when you hear the word* spirit? *Do you think of a wisp of vapor drifting across the sky? Does* spirit *mean the sort of thing that frightens children on Halloween? Is* spirit *just a formless nothingness to you?*

"To discover what spirit *really is, and what Jesus meant when He used that particular word, we must turn again to the Bible to the scene where Christ after His resurrection says: 'Handle Me, and see; for a*

*spirit hath not flesh and bones as ye see Me have'
(Luke 24:34).*

"Therefore we can be sure that spirit is without
*body. It is the exact opposite of body. Yet it has being
and power. This is difficult for us to understand
because we are trying to understand it with finite,
body-limited minds."[5]*

～

In the 1950s, Graham sometimes painted a frightening picture of God:

*"God is not a jolly fellow like Santa Claus; He is a
great bookkeeper. And he is keeping the book on you!
I am a Western Union boy! I have a death message! I
must tell you plainly—you are going to hell! You
listen! Don't you trifle with God! Don't you think you
can barter! You are a sinner! You have come short of
God's requirements! Your punishment is sure!"[6]*

～

*"God does not dwell in a body, so we cannot define
Him in a material way. God is a spirit. I have had
tremendous messages from Him, which are from the
Bible; it's not something I've dreamed up or had a
vision of. It's important to study the Bible on a daily
basis so He can speak to me."[7]*

～

*"God is not bound by body, yet He is a Person. He
feels. He thinks, He loves, He forgives, He sympa-
thizes with the problems and sorrows that we face."[8]*

~

"The Bible reveals Him as a Person. All through the Bible it says: 'God loves,' 'God says,' 'God does.' Everything that we attribute to a person is attributed to God. A person is one who feels, thinks, wishes, desires, and has all the expressions of personality."[9]

~

"Your finite mind is not capable of dealing with anything as great as the love of God. Your mind might have difficulty explaining how a black cow can eat green grass and give white milk—but you drink the milk and are nourished by it."[10]

~

"[God] is utterly perfect and absolute in every detail. He is too holy to touch sinful man, too holy to endure sinful living. He is a holy and perfect God."[11]

~

During the 1952 Washington, D.C., crusade, Graham was asked if God had stopped the rain to allow the rally on the steps of the Capitol to proceed. He replied: "I believe God does intervene. I also believe God did intervene today, as He has in days gone by when we have prayed concerning the matter of the weather." Then with a smile Billy noted: "But in all fairness, I have to remember that we prayed once out in Portland, Oregon, and it poured down."[12]

~

"It is the absence of the knowledge of God and man's refusal to obey Him that lies at the root of every problem that besets us."[13]

~

"Again and again—you cannot think your way to God, or use wisdom alone. You must use your heart."[14]

JESUS

Billy Graham's ministry, from the very beginning, has focused on a single message:

"Why is Christianity so different from every other religion in the world? The answer focuses not on a plan for living, but on the Person of Jesus Christ: Jesus, the Son of God the Father and the Second Person of the Trinity."[15]

~

Graham has an image of Jesus' face in his own mind. He says he thinks of Jesus as one who had "a very strong face and a very magnetic personality filled with tremendous charisma."[16]

~

"It is wrong to think of Jesus as a westerner. He was born and reared in that part of the world that touches Asia, Africa, and Europe. His skin was not as white as mine. He looked like the people who lived around him, Middle Eastern people."[17]

~

"The title 'Christ' means 'anointed one.' It is the term, in the Greek language, for the ancient Hebrew word 'Messiah'—the 'anointed one' whom God would send to save his people. Peter and the first believers of the early Christian Church recognized Jesus as the Messiah promised in the Old Testament."[18]

~

Billy Graham has never been one to challenge civil authority, which he explains is simply following the example of Jesus. After acceding to certain government restrictions on his preaching in Israel, he noted: "Jesus and Paul were also respectful of civil authority. Neither of them forced a confrontation with the Roman government on religious grounds, godless and decadent as it was, nor is that my calling as an evangelist."[19]

THE BIBLE

"Our call and power come from the infallible Word of God—the Bible. It is the very Scripture in which Jesus is revealed."[20]

~

"God caused the Bible to be written for the express purpose of revealing to man God's plan for his redemption. God caused this book to be written that He might make his everlasting laws clear to his children, and that they might have His great wisdom to

guide them and His great love to comfort them as
they make their way through life."[21]

~

"The more the archeologist digs and the more the
scientist discovers, the greater the confirmation of
the truth of the Bible."[22]

~

Early in his ministry, Graham began to doubt the veracity of the Bible. For six painful months he pondered whether the Bible could be trusted completely.

John Pollock explained in a biography of Graham: "After [preaching at] Altoona, Billy felt that he must decide once and for all either to spend his life studying whether or not God had spoken, or to spend it as God's ambassador, bringing a message which he might not fully comprehend in all details until after death. Must an intellectually honest man know everything about the Bible's origins before he could use it?"[23]

One day Graham dropped to his knees and prayed, "O God, there are many things in this book I do not understand. But, God, I am going to accept this book as your word *by faith*. I'm going to allow my faith to go beyond my intellect and believe that this is thy inspired word."[24]

Graham now describes the Bible as a book of faith, not necessarily a book of science.

~

In 1952 Graham accepted a copy of the new and controversial Revised Standard Version and told a crowd of 20,000 people: "These scholars have probably given us the most nearly perfect translation in English. While there may be room for disagreement in certain areas of the translation, yet this new version should supplement the King James version and make Bible reading a habit throughout America."

One of Graham's critics, David Cloud, notes that the evangelist almost single-handedly rescued another translation, *The Living Bible*, from oblivion. Cloud says: "*The Living Bible* might be called 'The Billy Graham Bible,' for it was he who made it the success that it is."[25]

Time magazine reported that Graham ordered 50,000 copies of *The Living Bible*. A short time later he ordered some 450,000 copies. Still later he ordered 600,000 special paperback versions for his autumn television crusade in 1972.[26]

∿

In 1987 Graham appeared in television ads for *The Book*, a condensed version of *The Living Bible*, saying it "reads like a novel."

In an advertisement in *Charisma* magazine, Graham said: "I read *The Living Bible* because in this book I have read the age-abiding truths of the scriptures with renewed interest and inspiration. *The Living Bible* communicates the message of Christ to our generation."[27]

~

Graham also has been criticized for his support for other newer translations of the Bible. David Cloud condemns "Graham's habit of honoring wicked, Bible-denying modernists."

Cloud contends that "Billy Graham has promoted practically every perverted Bible version to appear in the last four decades."

"*The Good News for Modern Man* (Today's English Version)," charges Cloud, "replaces the word 'blood' with 'death' in speaking of the atonement of Jesus Christ, and corrupted practically every passage dealing with Christ's deity. The translator of *The Good News for Modern Man*, Robert Bratcher, does not believe that Jesus Christ is God."[28]

PRAYER

"Prayer is more than a plea, it is a place where we must spend time if we are to learn its power."[29]

~

"If we have not learned to pray in our everyday lives, we will find it difficult to know God's peace and strength through prayer when the hard times come."[30]

~

"Jesus frequently prayed alone, separating Himself from every earthly distraction. I would strongly

urge you to select a place—a room or corner in your home, place of work, or in your yard or garden— where you can regularly meet God alone."[31]

~

"When we see the need of someone else, pray. When we know someone is in pain, pray. Let someone know you have prayed for them, and ask others to pray for you."[32]

~

"God is true to His word and answers all sincere prayers offered in the name of the Lord Jesus Christ."[33]

~

It grieved Graham when public prayer was no longer allowed in schools:

"After reading all this stuff in the Congressional Record *and all the arguments used against the prayer, I would say that every teacher in America has the right to stand up and read the Bible in front of the class. What has happened is the school boards and principals throughout the country have misinterpreted congressional intent. It would be good to have another poll because the American people, in my opinion by 92 percent, want prayer in the school."[34]*

~

Graham often quotes from the New Testament book of Thessalonians:

"Rejoice evermore. Pray without ceasing. In everything give thanks: for this is the will of God in Christ Jesus concerning you" (Thessalonians 5:16, 17, 18, King James version of the Holy Bible).

~

ANGELS

Long before angels became a fashionable topic for television shows and movies, Billy Graham talked of them. He often refers to the Old Testament book of Ezekiel, chapter 10, which contains a dramatic account of visitation by angels:

"And the cherubims lifted up their wings, and mounted up from the earth in my sights: when they went out, the wheels [of fire] also were beside them, and every one stood at the door of the east gate of the Lord's house; and the glory of God of Israel was over them above" (Ezekiel 10:19, King James Bible).

~

Angels play an important role, says Graham:

"They are God's messengers whose chief business is to carry out His orders in the world. He has given them an ambassadorial charge. He has designated and empowered them as holy deputies to perform works of righteousness."[35]

~

"God uses angels to work out the destinies of men and nations. He has altered the courses of the busy political and social areas of our society and directed the destinies of men by angels visitations many times over. We must be aware that angels keep in close and vital contact with all that is happening on the earth. Their knowledge of earthly matters exceeds that of men."[36]

HEAVEN

"Throughout every culture we have been led to the idea that we accept death as the end of life on earth. . . . Time bound as we are and goal oriented to achievements in our lifetime, we find it strange to anticipate heaven."[37]

∽

When he first starting preaching, Billy Graham presented an imaginative and literal view of heaven.

"We are going to sit around the fireplace and have parties, and the angels will wait on us, and we'll drive down the golden streets in a yellow Cadillac convertible."[38]

∽

In 1950, he said: "Heaven is as real as Los Angeles, London, Algiers or Boston. Heaven is 1600 miles long, 1600 miles wide, and 1600 miles high . . . as much as if you put Great Britain, Ireland, France, Spain,

Italy, Austria, Germany, and half of Russia in one place. That is how big the New Jerusalem is going to be. Boy, I can't wait until I get up there and look around."[39]

~

"Some people have speculated that [heaven is at] the North Star, but this is all speculative."[40]

~

By the late 1960s, Graham abandoned the colorful, literal descriptions of heaven that had characterized his sermons in the early 1950s:

"I believe . . . that there is an actual, literal heaven. I believe there's an actual literal hell. I . . . don't ask me where and don't ask me what it's going to look like and all of that. I don't know. I only know that Jesus warned us about one, and told us the joys and the happiness of the other."[41]

~

Decades later Graham explained: "I think heaven is going to be a place beyond anything we can imagine, or anyone in Hollywood, or Broadway can imagine. There is a passage in Revelation that says we will serve God in heaven. We're not going to have somebody fan us or sit around on a beach somewhere."[42]

~

"The same hand that made the beauty of this world has a more beautiful place prepared for us."[43]

~

"Everything in respect to heaven will be new. It is described as a new creation in which we shall move in new bodies, possessed of new names, singing new songs, living in a new city, governed by a new form of government, and challenged by new prospects of eternity."[44]

~

"Heaven will be the perfection we have always longed for. All the things that made earth unlovely and tragic will be absent in heaven. There will be no night, no death, no disease, no sorrow, no tears, no ignorance, no disappointment, no war. It will be filled with health, vigor, virility, knowledge, happiness, worship, love, and perfection."[45]

~

"Even when we allow our imaginations to run wild on the joys of heaven, we find that our minds are incapable of conceiving what it will be like."[46]

~

"How can we conceive of infinity? To imagine an existence that never ends is mind-boggling."[47]

~

Although Graham's ideas about heaven became more grand and less specific as time went on, he still has a sense of humor about heaven:

"I expect to spend eternity with God, the great, and the good—including Elvis Presley."[48]

～

On lost opportunity to go to heaven, Graham says:

"There is a videotape up in heaven, not only of your actions but of your thoughts as well. The meeting will be there and you will think 'O God, why didn't I take advantage of that night [Billy Graham preached] in Upton Park.'"[49]

～

Ruth Graham teases her husband that the afterlife may not be what he expects: "When Bill finds out that heaven is not like a Holiday Inn or a Marriott, he'll be back."[50]

THE DEVIL

"In his warfare against God, Satan uses the human race, which God created and loved. So God's forces of good and Satan's forces of evil have been engaged in a deadly conflict from the dawn of our history."[51]

～

"A well known pastor or evangelist is often a special target of Satan. The higher the visibility, the easier the target."[52]

～

Graham wonders if the devil didn't visit him in person during a 1970 crusade:

"Some 2,000 people came forward at the invitation, and I happened to look down and see a man standing down there, nicely dressed, with a neatly trimmed beard—but with the most evil face I've ever seen, right down there in front of me, doing this."

To demonstrate, Graham jumped from his chair, hunched his shoulders, rolled his eyes, and grimaced.

"That's what he was doing. And I couldn't help but wonder if he weren't trying to cast some Satanic spell over me, or over what was happening there."[53]

~

At a Chicago crusade in 1971, a group of Satan worshipers rushed past the ushers and ran down the aisles chanting.

"Don't worry about a thing, Dr. Graham, my police will handle it," said Mayor Richard Daley, who sat with Graham on the platform.

Graham responded, "Mr. Mayor, let me try it another way."

Graham went to the microphone and interrupted a hymn, saying: "There are 300 or 400 Satan worshipers here tonight. They've said that they're going to take over the platform. Now I'm going to ask you Christian young people to do something. Don't hurt them. Just surround them and love them and sing to them and, if you can, just gradually move them toward the doors."[54]

The Christian youth did as they were asked, and soon the hall was cleared of the intruders.

"My," said Mayor Daley, "I ought to have you in all these riots we're having around here."[55]

HELL

"There is a heaven and a hell, though I cannot describe them completely and accurately. The Bible teaches very clearly and unmistakably that hell is that word that describes the judgment of all who are finally separated from God. And it cannot be otherwise, because man was created to have fellowship with God, and if he finally cuts himself off from that fellowship, he can never possibly be happy."[56]

⁓

"The only thing I could say for sure is that hell means separation from God. We are separated from His light, from His fellowship. That is going to hell. When it comes to a literal fire, I don't preach it because I'm not sure about it."[57]

⁓

"Will a loving God send a man to hell? The answer from Jesus and the teachings of the Bible is, clearly, 'Yes!' He does not send man willingly, but man condemns himself to eternal hell because in his blind-

ness, stubbornness, egotism, and love of sinful plea-
sure, he refuses God's way of salvation and the hope
of eternal life with Him."[58]

SIN

"Why many people think the 'forbidden fruit'
was an apple I have never been able to understand.
The Bible does not specifically state what kind
of fruit was on the forbidden tree, but the tree itself
was called 'the tree of the knowledge' of good and
evil."[59]

~

"It is the presence of sin that prevents man from
being happy. It is because of sin that man has never
been able to obtain the utopia of which he dreams.
Every project, every civilization that he builds ulti-
mately fails and falls into oblivion because man's
works are all wrought in unrighteousness. The ruins
[of civilized life] around us at this moment are elo-
quent witness to the sin that fills the world."[60]

~

"There is a difference between sin *and* sins. *There is*
sin *(singular), which is the heart of our spiritual*
disease, and there are sins *(plural), which are the*
fruit or signs of the disease. If I spent all of my time
on sins *(plural), I might never be able to get at*
the root cause, which is sin *(singular). The Lord*

Jesus Christ died on the cross to deal with sin, *and not just individual* sins.*"61*

∽

David Frost asked Graham if taking a drink was a sin. The evangelist replied:

"I don't think the Bible teaches teetotalism. When the Bible says that Jesus turned water into wine, that wasn't grape juice, in my judgment. That was wine, the best wine. And I think that the Scripture teaches in the last chapter of Proverbs, for example, when a person has troubles in an old age and so forth that it's good to take some alcohol. Or it says—Paul was writing to Timothy and said take a little wine for your stomach's sake. You'd be amazed at how many people have stomach trouble and use that to justify it, you see.

"But the reason that I don't [drink], David, is because I feel that I have another principle at work. The Bible says, if I do anything to make my brother stumble or fall, then I'm not to do it. And if people saw me sitting at a table drinking [alcohol] in America at least—then they may say, 'Well, Billy Graham does it; it's all right for me.' and they may become an alcoholic as a result of that. So I have to be careful of my witness."62

∽

"A thought enters; we pamper it; it germinates and grows into an evil act."63

~

When asked about the troubles of TV evangelists Jim and Tammy Bakker and Jimmy Swaggart, Graham says: "We are all tempted. I think if they had realized what was happening and turned to the Lord in the deepest part of their lives, they would not have fallen. Of course, when a person becomes what [the Bakkers and Jimmy Swaggart] were on television and becomes a celebrity, he faces a special kind of temptation, a special time of vulnerability because you become a target for anybody who is jealous or anybody who is disloyal in the organization."[64]

~

On being asked by David Frost in what ways he has yielded to temptation, Graham responded:

"I suppose, David, in almost every way. I have yielded, primarily in my thinking processes. I have never committed adultery. I have never, and I'm not saying it boastfully, I'm saying that because I think God kept me. I never touched a woman in the wrong way before I was married. I've never touched a woman in the wrong way. And I think God himself has protected me. But there were times when the temptation was great. A few times. Especially since I've been married, when I traveled in other parts of the world. I was with a friend of mine, who was a great Christian leader and he became so overwhelmed by temptation that he not only took cold showers, but he took the keys to his

room and threw them out the window. It was in Paris. He didn't want to be able to get out of his room."[65]

When asked several years later what temptations he did succumb to, Graham answered:

"I think that the number one sin that a man can have is pride. That was Satan's sin. That's the greatest sin. Idolatry and pride and they go together. I suppose there's been that, but I'm not conscious of it. Because today I feel the opposite. I feel like I'm nothing but a worm crawling along the floor and shouldn't have any recognition from God at all, except judgment because I feel that my life has been a failure in many ways."[66]

⌒

But temptation alone isn't enough to corrupt a Christian, Graham says.

"Temptation is natural. Temptation is not sin. It is yielding to temptation that is sin. God never brings temptations to us. He allows it to test us. Temptation is the work of the devil."[67]

⌒

A violation of one of the Ten Commandments is a sin, says Graham, regardless of which commandment is violated:

"The Seventh Commandment [thou shalt not commit adultery] is just one of ten. The sin of immorality,

although God loathes it, is no worse than lying or cheating."⁶⁸

~

The guilt of sin can last a very long time:

"I can think of a time right now that I told my father a lie. That's always bothered me. In fact it's bothered me very much, because it was quite a big lie that I told him at one time."⁶⁹

~

"I am not the holy, righteous prophet of God that many people think I am. I share with [Reformation leader John] Wesley the feeling of my own inadequacy and sinfulness constantly. I am often amazed that God can use me at all."⁷⁰

DEATH

Velma Barfield was convicted of poisoning three people and was sentenced to die. Graham's daughter Anne Lotz spent many hours counseling and praying with Barfield.

On the day of Barfield's execution, Billy Graham called her on the phone saying: "Velma, you're going to beat us home. Tomorrow night you'll be in the arms of Jesus."

Barfield, who had become a Christian while in prison, responded: "Praise the Lord."

Following the execution, Graham went to the North

Carolina Correctional Institute for Women where Barfield was executed and visited her cell.

The warden told him: "You know, since Velma's death, I just couldn't bring myself to come in here. On the night of her execution, she was the happiest, the most radiant human being I ever met."

While at the prison, Graham held a service and at the invitation to come forward for Christ, 200 people responded, including several guards.[71]

～

"Now, the Bible teaches that to be absent from the body is to be present with the Lord. The moment a Christian dies, he goes immediately into the presence of Christ. There his soul awaits the resurrection, when the soul and body will be rejoined. Many people ask, 'How can the bodies that have decayed and been cremated be raised?' Scientists have already proved that no chemicals disappear from the earth. The God who made the body in the first place can bring all the original chemicals back together again, and the body will be raised to join the soul. But the new body that we will have will be a glorious body like unto the body of Christ. It will be an eternal body. It will never know tears, heartache, tragedy, disease, suffering, or death."[72]

～

"Death is not natural, for man was created to live and not to die. It is the result of God's judgment because of man's sin and rebellion. Without God's

grace through Christ, it is a gruesome spectacle. I have stood at the bedside of people dying without Christ; it was a terrible experience. I have stood at the bedside of those who were dying in Christ; it was a glorious experience."[73]

~

"When my maternal grandmother died, for instance, the room seemed to fill with a heavenly light. She sat up in bed and almost laughingly said, 'I see Jesus. He has his arms outstretched towards me. I see Ben [her husband who had died some years earlier] and I see the angels.' She slumped over, absent from the body but present with the Lord."[74]

~

"Most of the supernatural experiences we hear or read about have classic similarities. The person who is 'dead' rises out of his or her body, hears strange sounds, seems to be going down a long, dark tunnel and recognizes himself hovering somewhere between life and death, and then encounters someone or something in white, or a diffusion of light. Those who return from this journey are changed persons. These kinds of stories are not an American phenomenon. They are described by people of other cultures and nations."[75]

~

"I'm looking forward to death, I'll be very happy to get out of this body and into the new world that's

being prepared. It'll be a feeling of tremendous joy and relief and rest. The Bible says I have not seen nor heard, nor has there entered the mind of man, what God has in store for us in the future life."[76]

~

"Of course, I have the natural *tensions and fears of self-preservation, because if we didn't have them we might walk in front of a truck or something else, but that's not because I'm afraid. Many times I look forward to death. I have no fear of death whatsoever."*[77]

~

"The truth is that all of us have our time to die, and the conspiracy of silence that so often surrounds death today cannot change that fact. . . . within most of us is a strong desire to hold on to physical life as long as possible."[78]

~

"Most of us have a subliminal desire to leave this world with some degree of dignity. . . . Quick, quiet, easy. But life doesn't follow the pattern we have so clumsily designed . . . death has many faces and voices."[79]

~

"We get death threats quite often, and I pay absolutely no attention to them. I have no bodyguards, and I don't have anybody protecting me like that. And they're just put aside and I feel that

I'm clothed in the armor of God, and I'll go on as long as God wants me to, and if He wants me killed, I'm happy to be killed."[80]

ARMAGEDDON

Stephen Olford, a longtime friend of the evangelist, once pointed out: "Unless there was a crisis somewhere, Billy couldn't preach. In the midst of one crusade, I remember him walking down the street one afternoon and buying four newspapers just in the space of one block, looking for a crisis. He'd snatch one up and rummage hurriedly through it, then pitch it away and grab another. A fellow walking along with us finally turned to me and whispered, 'Stephen, he's thrown down every one of those newspapers—he can't find a crisis anywhere; he's not going to be able to preach tonight."[81]

$\sim$

In most cases Graham has been able to find a crisis. He has consistently preached that Armageddon—the return of Jesus Christ—could occur at any moment and that terrible events are precursors of the end. Accounts of the end of the world appear several places in the Bible:

"And ye shall hear of wars and rumors of wars; see that ye be not troubled; for all these things must come to pass, but the end is not yet. For nations shall rise against nations, and kingdom and against kingdom; and there shall be famines, and pestilences, and earthquakes, in divers places. All these are the beginning of sorrows" (Matthew 24:6, 7, and 8 in the King James version of the Holy Bible).

~

In 1965:

"We are like a people under sentence of death, waiting for the date to be set. We sense that something is about to happen. We know that things cannot go on as they are. History has reached an impasse. We are now on a collision course. Something is about to give. The flames are licking all around our world—the roof is about to cave in—man is caught in a fire raging out of control."[82]

~

In 1977:

"The atomic clock at the University of Chicago was recently moved from 12 minutes before midnight to 9 minutes until midnight. How much longer can the world have until destruction comes? We see time collapsing all about us."[83]

~

In 1982:

"We know that things cannot go on as they are. History is about to reach an impasse. Many world leaders now feel that the world is on a collision course with catastrophe, both economically and militarily. Something seems about to give. The world crisis presses in around us, making us want to

61

escape. We wish it were just a bad dream that will be gone when we awaken tomorrow—but there is no escape."[84]

~

In 1992:

"In my book World Aflame *[1965], I spoke of the 1960s and 1970s as a time of anger and outrage, as a warfare of conflicting ideologies. While the circumstances of our own time may have changed superficially, I am convinced that the greater social dimensions have not really changed at all. In fact, we are still paying the price for the recklessness of the free-thinking sixties. More than ever before, our culture is caught in a web of irresponsibility and self-centeredness. Our society is still trapped in the same conditions of desperation and fear that have been propelling us downward recklessly into an emotional inferno."[85]*

In his 1992 book *Storm Warning*, Graham sounded a similar alarm:

"Editorials in the international press are even gloomier than those in American newspapers. Constantly the words 'Armageddon' and 'Apocalypse' are used to describe events on the world scene. A decade ago, George Orwell's gloomy book 1984 *was the image everyone used. Today Orwell's fiction seems pale in comparison to the reality: What we fear today is the Apocalypse itself."[86]*

For those who aren't saved, says Graham, the conse-
quences will be dire:

> *"Don't make the mistake of thinking that because
> God is Love that everything is going to be sweet,
> beautiful, and happy and that no one will be pun-
> ished for his sins. God's holiness demands that all sin
> be punished, but God's love provides the plan and
> way of redemption for sinful men. God's love pro-
> vided the cross of Jesus, by which man can have for-
> giveness and cleansing."*[87]

> *"Westminster Abbey and St. Peter's Basilica in
> Rome have great altars with marble crypts beneath
> them. Imagine such a church at midnight when it
> is dark and silent. The tombs of the saints and mar-
> tyrs lie sealed as they have been for centuries. Then
> suddenly, seals break, coffins spring open, stones roll
> away, and hundreds, maybe thousands, of spirits
> pour into the Cathedral, all crying out with one
> voice, 'How long Sovereign Lord? How long until we
> are avenged?'"*[88]

> *"Ultimately, the Bible looks into the future to foresee
> a new world in which peace and righteousness pre-
> vail. There is to be world peace. There is to be a new
> social order. There is to be a new age. There is to be
> a completely new man in whom there will be no false*

pride, hate, lust, greed, or prejudice. This will be the climax of human history."[89]

∼

Graham suggests that there will be some surprises at the time of the Apocalypse:

"It's going to be quite a revealing thing at the last judgment when we see everyone standing naked before God."[90]

DOUBTS

Although Billy Graham sometimes doubts his own abilities, his own effectiveness, he seems to have no doubt about his religion.

"The Christian life is not a constant high. I have my moments of deep discouragement. I have to go to God in prayer with tears in my eyes, and say, 'O God, forgive me,' or 'Help me.'"[91]

∼

How does Graham feel every time he mounts the stage for a sermon?

"I'm always afraid, afraid that I may give the wrong word to someone and that it might affect their eternal destiny. I worry every time I go to the platform that I'm unworthy to be there. I often wish that the platform would just open up and drop me through."[92]

∼

Despite his accomplishments, Graham says:

"I have in many ways failed ... I haven't lived a life of devotion, meditation, and prayer. I've allowed the world to creep into my life too much."[93]

∼

"If anything bothers me, it is the thought that at Judgment Day I may find that I have not been as faithful as some other minister who is slugging it out day after day with few visible achievements in a storefront in Harlem."[94]

∼

In 1972, *The Saturday Evening Post* observed that Graham's deeply based beliefs are the source of his strength: "His emotional power, even held to a calmly conversational level, is hypnotic. But the main impression is of a man secure in what he believes, who has not wavered over the years, and who never will. That kind of inner strength is awesome."[95]

∼

BILLY GRAHAM'S WORK

MISSION

Billy Graham has been accused of skirting social issues such as poverty and race problems in his sermons and other activities. But to Graham, his mission is simple and focused. His job is to convert as many people as possible to Christianity.

"Contrary to the opinion of some, the evangelist is not primarily a social reformer, a temperance lecturer, or a moralizer. He is simply a keryx, *a proclaimer of the good news, which in capsule form is 'Christ died for our sins according to the Scriptures . . . was buried . . . rose again the third day, according to the Scriptures (I Cor. 15:3f.)."*[1]

"The term 'evangelist' comes from a Greek word meaning 'one who announces good news.'"[2]

"[The evangelist's] primary message centers in the death, burial, and resurrection of Christ, His coming

again, and the need for all men everywhere to repent and believe."³

⁓

The Archbishop of Canterbury's Committee of 1918 said that "To evangelize is to present Christ Jesus in the power of the Holy Spirit that men shall come to put their trust in God through Him, to accept Him as their Savior and serve Him as their King in the fellowship of His Church."⁴

⁓

In 1946 representatives of 20 Protestant denominations called the Federal Council of Churches, worked out this definition of evangelism: "Evangelism is the presentation of the good news of God in Jesus Christ so that men are brought through the power of the Holy Spirit to put their trust in God, accept Jesus Christ as their Savior from the guilt and power of sin, to follow and serve Him as their Lord in the fellowship of the church and in the vocations of the common life."⁵

⁓

"My one purpose in life is to help people find a personal relationship with God, which, I believe, comes through knowing Christ."⁶

⁓

"As long as there is a soul to be won to Christ, I'm under orders by the Lord to go try to win that soul to Christ."⁷

～

"Evangelism's like an arrow. There's a sharp point, which is the gospel. But then an arrow broadens in many different styles. There are many effective methods in evangelism. But they all depend on the Holy Spirit. And we often have difficulty measuring the relative effectiveness of each, at least right away."[8]

～

"God does the saving, I'm told to preach Christ as the only way to salvation. But it is God who is going to do the judging, not Billy Graham."[9]

～

"Whether the story of Christ is told in a huge stadium, across the desk of some powerful leader, or shared with a golfing companion, it satisfies a common hunger. All over the world, whenever I meet people face to face, I am made aware of this personal need among the famous and successful as well as the lonely and obscure."[10]

～

"Indeed, sometimes evangelists have been ignored or opposed by churches, as in the case of John Wesley, whose mission was rejected by his own church. Despite this, in almost every generation God has raised up evangelists, who often have had to pursue their calling outside the structured church."[11]

～

"Some who obviously had the gift of evangelism have modestly subdued their gift because they are afraid of being accused of nonintellectualism, emotionalism, commercialism, or being too concerned with statistics. These are the subtleties of Satan to keep the man with the gift of evangelism from being used."[12]

～

Asked if he has some sort of special talent, Billy Graham answers:

"Yes, at the invitation. I believe that there is a gift that God has given me in asking people to come forward and make a commitment to Christ at the end of my sermons. And in the 5 minutes or the 10 minutes that this appeal lasts, when I'm standing there, not saying a word, it's when most of my strength leaves me. I cannot explain that. I don't usually get tired quickly. But I get tired in the invitation. This is when I become exhausted. I don't know what it is, but something is going out at the moment."[13]

～

Graham was asked at a press conference during his 1954 London crusade: "What do you know about the suffering of Christ that you preach about so often? You have never really suffered have you? You have lived fairly well, with most of the comforts of life, it would seem...." At this point Graham cut the reporter off:

"When a Western Union messenger boy delivers a death message to a home, he doesn't take part himself in all the suffering connected with that message. He just delivers the telegram, that's all."[14]

~

Carl F. H. Henry, editor of Graham's *Christianity Today* magazine, said that "Graham is not simply an evangelist, but is expressly an evangelical evangelist, and that implies at once an irreducible theological content and commitment to a complex of Bible doctrines. He has never vacillated on the fundamentals that evangelical orthodoxy championed against theological liberalism. When modernist and humanist critics accused him of turning back the clock of theological progress by a generation, he offered to escort them back 19 centuries to Jesus and the apostles."[15]

~

It is said that no man is a hero at his own kitchen table. Ruth Graham, on being asked why God chose Graham to be such a spiritual force, quipped: "Maybe it's because he doesn't have all that many natural talents."[16]

~

To others who would follow in his footsteps and become evangelists, Graham says:

"The task of evangelism seems humanly impossible—but 'with God all things are possible.' The disciples did their part, and within a generation that little

band had grown until groups of Christians were to be found throughout much of the Roman Empire. They were changed from a dispirited, bewildered group of men to a fearless team of evangelists who were willing to go anywhere, do anything, and sacrifice anything 'for the sake of the gospel.' No wonder it was said that the early Christians had 'turned the world upside down.'"[17]

∽

"I read recently that there are about 100 organizations planning to evangelize the whole world by the year 2000. I wish them the best; but no matter how good a job they do, there will still be more. Every generation needs re-evangelizing."[18]

∽

Graham has devoted much of his time and his organization's money to help develop evangelism worldwide. For example, in 1986 he invited 8,000 itinerant preachers from around the world to Amsterdam for a 10-day international conference. It cost $21 million to stage the massive training session.[19]

THE CRUSADES: LOS ANGELES, LONDON, AND NEW YORK

"What an hour for the proclamation of His gospel! This is the time to make Christ known, whether we be pastor, teacher, evangelist or layman."[20]

Billy Graham has preached to some 210 million people in 185 countries, during his more than 350 crusades. He says:

"I don't know why God has allowed me to have this, I'll have to ask him when I get to heaven."[21]

~

Graham started as an evangelist with Youth for Christ, a nationwide program for teenagers. Gradually his crusades expanded, and in 1949 he burst upon the American consciousness with a flamboyantly successful series of tent meetings in Los Angeles.

NOTE: For more on the Los Angeles Crusade, see the section "Billy Converts a Mobster and Is Discovered by a Nation."

~

The London 1954 crusade was Graham's first foray abroad, and it was not an easy beginning. The Billy Graham Greater London Crusade ran into rough water even before he arrived. He set sail on the ship the *United States* for Great Britain in February 1954, confident that with the support of President Dwight D. Eisenhower, Britain's Evangelical Alliance, the Salvation Army, and the Plymouth Brethren, the crusade would be well received.

However, when three days out from Southampton he learned that the English press had reacted negatively to the enormous public relations barrage that his publicity manager, Gerald Beavan, had put in motion.

The London *Evening News* called Graham an "American hot gospel specialist who was 'actor-manager of the show'" and warned that "like a Biblical Baedeker, he takes his listeners strolling down Pavements of Gold, introduces them to rippling-muscled Christ, who resembles Charles Atlas with a halo, then drops them abruptly into the Lake of Fire for a sample scalding."[22]

~

A brochure sent by Graham's people to a small group of wealthy American backers of the first London crusade seemed to suggest that the British had lost their historic faith. The brochure declared that when the war ended, a sense of disillusionment and frustration gripped England, and what Hitler's bombs could not destroy, socialism was ending.

London *Daily Herald* columnist Hannen Swaffer demanded to know what evils Graham referred to: "The abolition of the Poor Law, the National Health Service, town planning, family allowances, improved educational facilities?"

He insisted that Graham "apologize, or stay away." Labour member of Parliament Geoffrey de Freitas suggested that Graham was "interfering in British politics under the guise of religion" and announced plans to challenge Graham's admission to England.[23]

Graham immediately assured the editor of the *Daily Herald* that it was all a "horrible mistake" and that the key word should have read *secularism* rather than *socialism*.

～

If Graham's first crusade abroad had failed, his entire ministry might have taken a different direction. Yet he received warm welcomes from many people. As he passed through customs, an official greeted him, "Welcome to England, and good luck, sir, we need you." A dockworker said, "I'm praying for you, sir." A soldier Graham met along the way said, "God bless you, sir."[24]

～

Yet with the cool reception by the press, Billy and his team expected almost no one to turn up at the Harringay Arena. Billy prayed earnestly that the Lord might somehow help to make the crusade a success. As he and Ruth approached the arena on the first night, it appeared there was practically no one entering. He said to Ruth: "Honey, let's just go and face it and believe God had a purpose in it."

As they reached the door Willis Haymaker, a member of the Graham organization, rushed out. "The arena is jammed!" he exclaimed.

"What do you mean, jammed?" asked Billy. "We didn't see anybody as we approached."

"The main entrance is on the other side," said Haymaker. "Most of the traffic and people came from that direction. The place is full and running over, and hundreds are outside."[25]

～

Despite the crowds, the official reception remained cool. After attending one of Graham's London sermons, the Reverend Frank Martin wrote in the *Sunday Graphic*: "This Billy Graham line just won't do! . . . Just pelting us with texts will never convert British sinners. The whole thing is (and I say it in all charity) too spiritually bouncy and immature."[26]

At least one reporter found Graham completely disarming. "He seems to have the sincerity, ingenuousness, the sort of simple charm that is the greatest fun about Americans and the quality that makes us love Danny Kaye so," she said.[27]

The established religious and news media aside, Brits rushed to hear Graham.

∼

Graham soon had to move his sermons to the larger Wembley Stadium, where he preached to audiences of up to 185,000 people, the largest crowd ever assembled in Britain for a religious event. Working with local people, the Graham team wired up a number of facilities in other cities, increasing the audiences for Billy's sermons to 400,000 people.

The Bishop of Barking, one of the major sponsors for the Graham's London crusade, had been heavily criticized by the press for supporting the evangelist. He told Graham, "If you've been made to appear a fool for Christ's sake, then I'm happy to appear a fool with you."[28]

∼

The country manners of Graham and some of his people amused Londoners. Just after a sermon at Wembley Stadium, where 2,000 people responded to Graham's invitation to accept the teachings of Jesus Christ, the Archbishop of Canterbury said to Grady Wilson, "We'll never see a sight like that again until we get to heaven."

"That's right, Brother Archbishop," Wilson responded.[29]

Queen Elizabeth II came to Graham's defense when a British chaplain asked Graham if conversions at his crusades "stick." Recalled a Graham associate, "As quick as a flash, Her Majesty spat out, 'Sir, of *course* they stick.'"[30]

NOTE: A study conducted by Graham's organization in 1988 indicated that approximately 75 percent of people who answered the altar call remained Christians.

Billy preached every night for three months, expending so much energy he lost 22 pounds. At the end of the crusade, even the harumphing Reverend Martin wrote: "Thank you, Billy. You've done us a power of good. Come again soon."[31]

The magazine *Christian Century*, frequently critical of Billy Graham, noted that while Graham did a lot of biblical teaching in London, the evangelist also learned and grew from the experience.

⌣

Graham did indeed learn important lessons:

"When I stand up to preach, in one sense I am not primarily concerned—and this may sound irreverent—whether anybody responds or not. All I am is a mouthpiece giving God's message, and it is up to Him to perform the work in the hearts of the people. If they reject Him, it is their responsibility before God, not mine. And so I no longer carry that great load that was breaking me down physically."[32]

⌣

During the London crusade of 1954, Ruth Graham told of an overly friendly man who approached her in Hyde Park. "I'm busy tonight," she told the man.

He then asked her out the next night.

"I'm busy then too," she told him.

And the next?

"Yes I'm busy then too."

"Just what is it that keeps you busy every night? he asked.

"I go to hear Billy Graham speak at the Harringay Arena," she said.

"You wouldn't be *related* to Billy Graham, would you?" he asked.

"Yes," she said. "I'm his wife."

"Oh my. . . . "[33]

～

Graham continued his missions abroad, often startling people of other cultures with his fast-paced, dynamic style of preaching. In his 1954 crusade in West Germany, German papers dubbed Graham as "God's Machine Gun."[34]

～

The next year, 1955, Graham took his message to Scotland. During that six-week crusade Graham reckons he reached some 500,000 people.

Billy and Ruth were invited to a dinner as guests of the Duke of Hamilton at the palace of Holyroodhouse in Edinburgh. It seemed to Graham that almost everyone there was a lord or a lady. Billy said to a handsome young man in black tie and tuxedo:

"Your Grace, I don't believe I've met you."

"No, sir, you haven't. I'm your waiter this evening, and you might like to know, sir, that *Your Grace* is reserved for dukes and archbishops."[35]

～

In 1957 Billy Graham conducted a grueling 16-week crusade in New York City. On the final day of the crusade he spoke outside at Times Square on the so-called Great White Way, the crossroads of the world. It was the hundredth meeting of the crusade, and 125,000 people showed up, completely filling the square and spilling over on to Sixth and Seventh avenues. Films of the event show men in suits and broad ties and women dressed up with pillbox hats and strands of choker pearls, the height of style for the day.

Graham himself appeared as a towering icon, preaching with magnetism, passion, and certainty. The contrast is striking when compared to the 80-year-old Graham of 1998, whose crusades in Canada and Florida were broadcast worldwide. The early Graham stood like a massive, jagged rock; the Graham of today is more like the Rock of Ages, gently worn down and softened by the years, unyielding in his faith and with his inner strength still intact.[36]

Celebrities or well-known public figures often join Graham on stage. In New York that year, both Richard Nixon and radio personality Paul Harvey were guests. When Graham held another New York crusade in 1969, the beloved college football coach Bear Bryant was his guest.

～

Critics of the 1957 event suggested that the New York crusade was less effective because a large number of the converts were already church members. To Graham, a renewal or recommitment to Christianity can be as important as a person's original conversion.

> *"If I were not convinced that large numbers of the inquirers actually are transformed by Christ in our crusades, I would retire to my mountain home and spend the rest of my days writing devotional literature for armchair Christians."*[37]

～

Despite the apparent success of Graham's subsequent 1969 New York crusade, *Commonweal* magazine said: "His Crusade team exhibited the technical and managerial proficiency worthy of any first rate, multimillion dollar corporation . . . they were in New York to save souls in large numbers and planned to use the most efficient, effective method to bring the Word of God to a city of 8 million. As one flyer announced, 'Billy Graham is able to preach to more people on one telecast than the Apostle Paul reached in his lifetime.'

"By failing to speak to the meaning of the City he doomed any chance of touching the uncommitted. So, in the end, despite his efforts, Graham failed to reach the group he came to speak to and failed to dent the life-style of the town. If the Graham Crusade failed to spark the fire of faith, it wasn't for lack of salesmanship. The people decided they just didn't want the product."[38]

～

Jimmy Karam of Little Rock, Arkansas, a hard-nosed segregationist who responded to Graham's invitation to accept Christ at a New York crusade, explained his own position: "I had tried all my life to live a decent life. But when I accepted Jesus Christ into my life, he took away drinking, smoking, gambling, running around and all the things I couldn't do for myself. He did it just like that. That is what is so wonderful about Billy Graham's ministry. I don't care how many kings or queens he had been with, Billy Graham has saved lives such as mine all over the world. And that is what he lives for; he lives to see lost people find salvation through Christ and then to help us grow in Christ."[39]

～

The Sydney, Australia, *Daily Mirror* reported a local magistrate as saying "The Billy Graham Crusade has cut crime rate in parts of Sydney by an estimated 50 percent."[40]

～

In 1982 the Russian Orthodox Church planned an international peace conference. Billy Graham was invited to speak and accepted with three conditions: One, he would go only as an observer, not a full delegate. That way, if the conference ended with a political pro-Soviet pronouncement, Graham would not be part of it. Second, he insisted that he is able to speak on any biblical topic he chose. Third, he wanted to be allowed to preach in two Moscow churches.

Still, Graham was not certain that he was doing the right thing. He contacted former President Nixon for advice, who assured him the Soviet government would use him for their own propaganda purposes. However, Nixon urged Graham to go. Although the U.S. ambassador to the Soviet Union strongly opposed the trip, Graham decided to accept:

"I will have my own 'propaganda'—the gospel— and it's more powerful."[41]

～

When Graham stepped off the plane in Moscow, a group of reporters handed him envelopes.

"What are these?" he asked.

"Letters from the Siberian Pentecostals,"[42] replied a newsman. Four years earlier two families had taken refuge in the American embassy, on the grounds that they were being persecuted for their faith. The letters contained demands the Siberians were making on the Soviets and on Graham. Graham, caught off guard, had no comment. Later he was chastised for not speaking out for the two families. Under any circumstances confrontation, especially with governments, is not Graham's approach to solving problems.

"I knew that if I publicly castigated the Soviet government for its policies, I would never have another chance to meet privately with the only people—the leaders—who could bring about change."[43]

On Saturday evening Graham was taken to see two Moscow churches. They were packed. Graham made an off-the-cuff comment that it took devotion not often found in American churches to pack a church on a Saturday night. When the comment was reported in American newspapers, the implication was that Graham had said Russians were more devout than Americans.

~

Graham has been so worn out from crusades that he has slept for two days straight after coming home:

"It's like being in a hurricane, and all of a sudden it stops and there is nothing but quiet."[44]

~

Once Graham returned home after a particularly exhausting crusade. He was picked up at a Georgia airport by his associate, T. W. Wilson, and promptly fell asleep in the backseat of the car.

An hour later Wilson stopped for gasoline. Graham woke up and stepped out of the car to stretch his legs. Wilson got back in the car and drove off, thinking Graham was still asleep in the back. He arrived in Montreat only to find that Graham was missing.

In the meantime, Graham went to a coffeeshop next to the service station and asked the owner if he could find him a ride home. The owner asked his name, and Graham, wearing dark glasses, an old golf cap, and rumpled clothes, responded, "Why, I'm Billy Graham."

The owner replied, "Yes, and I'm George Washington."

Graham had to call the proprietor of a local motel whom he knew to arrange a ride home.[45]

NOTE: A full list of the cities and countries where Billy Graham has led crusades can be found at the back of the book.

~ ✷ ~

THE BILLY GRAHAM PLAN

Every Billy Graham Crusade begins with an invitation from a group of concerned Christians who believe their community is in need of a religious revival. The Billy Graham Evangelistic Association (BGEA) receives some

500 invitations for crusades each year. At its peak, the organization staged four to five crusades annually, but in recent years Graham's health limits the number of appearances that he personally is able to make. A lot of work goes into sifting through the invitations to select the most worthy, those with adequate facilities, and those most ready to put the crusade on.

One member of the crusade team said that smaller cities have little chance of having Graham preach there, although BGEA does sometimes send other popular evangelists to smaller venues. "Most realize their towns are just not large enough to turn down Chicago for. Take Charleston, West Virginia. Charleston is a big city and they would really like Dr. Graham, but it's impossible because Charleston doesn't—well, it would be like taking a four-row cotton picker into a five-acre cotton field. You'd be foolish to waste the time."[46]

Having made a tentative selection, the Billy Graham Plan goes into action. BGEA sends an advance person out to the city that has requested a crusade. This advance person works with local religious organizations to generate enthusiasm for the project and explain how the financial aspects will work.

The crusades are organized jointly by local religious organizations and churches, sometimes local business and political people, along with the Graham team.

Christianity Today contributor Martin Marty says that the local organization is one of the strengths of a Graham crusade. Many fundamentalist churches would be possessive about their own meetings and the people who were converted there. But "Graham would refuse to come to your town unless there was a broad 'church federation' backing. He would not like to be on stage unless the United Methodists bishop or even, he has hoped since 1965, the Catholic bishop was there, too."[47]

BGEA proposes a budget for the crusade, and a local executive committee is set up to manage the project and the budget. Typically the local churches are responsible for raising and administering the funds, paying all the advertising, printing, postage, staff housing, and the like. They also provide the ushers, choir, counselors, and prayer group leaders.

The goal is to raise about one-third of the projected expenses before the crusade starts. Graham himself will sometimes help by holding fund-raising breakfasts or luncheons, at which he himself appears. This activity may precede the crusade by a year or even two.

BGEA supplies a professional team to help pull off the event itself. The team is composed of a publicity person, counseling experts, a business advisor, a choir director, soloist and other entertainers, piano player/organist, and assistant evangelists. Mostly these are salaried BGEA staff members. Two offerings are taken during the crusade and whatever surplus is left after expenses have been paid go to BGEA.

For each crusade funds are raised locally. Afterward the finances are audited, and the audit results are published in the local newspapers.

In 1975, a writer described the people attending a Billy Graham service this way:

"The crowd filing in is happy, well ordered, rather quiet, but not subdued—a cross-section of 'middle America.' There are some beards and beads, but most wear that scrubbed, apple-pie look so often associated with 'the typical American,' and so often described as 'wholesome.' There are quite a few blacks and browns, and a whole section of Spanish speaking. Everybody is polite, friendly and good humored, many carrying Bibles, as they have been asked to do."[48]

All of Graham's crusade services follow a similar pattern. They start with music, followed by prayer, and then Graham's sermon, followed by the invitation to make a commitment to Christ. In most crusades approximately 4 to 5 percent of the attendees come forward at Graham's invitation. The number of people Graham can reach during a crusade has increased over the years. Now arenas are connected electronically to other halls or facilities and the service is broadcast live on radio or television. These offsite services do not appear to have reduced the percentage of commitments to Christ for each event.

Converts fill out decision cards at the end of the service. These cards are processed by up to 70 volunteer workers, who begin work immediately after the service and continue until they are done, even into the small hours of the next morning. Local churches then contact these converts for follow-up.

Graham's daughter Anne Lotz explains, "Daddy's is one of the most effective and complex evangelistic organizations in the world."[49]

~ ✳ ~

MONEY AND WHAT TO DO WITH IT

Graham got into a hotel elevator with a man who said, "Has anyone ever told you you look a lot like Billy Graham?"

"A lot of people have," Graham replied.

"Well, I'd sure like to have his money," the man said.[50]

～

Graham once said that although money came easily, he'd never been tempted to live lavishly.

"No, I never have. I don't know why, but I determined years ago that I was not going to go for the money. I've never been interested in money, except as it pays our expenses and bills and things like that. And my wife and I could have been millionaires many times over. We've been offered everything you can think of, and we have said no to all of them."[51]

～

An incident early in Graham's career made him understand that the money from his crusades had to be handled very carefully. The image of wrong-doing, he realized, can be as potent as wrong-doing itself.

"In the early days I, like most other traveling evangelists, financed crusades by receiving love offerings. After a crusade like Los Angeles, Portland, or Atlanta, the people would give a love offering. After the Atlanta crusade, though, one of the Atlanta papers printed a picture of me getting into a convertible and waving my hat. Next to that was a photo of a great big bag of money—my love offering. Cliff [Barrows] and I used to divide the love offering. I think the highest amount I ever got was $18,000. But that was big money in those days for

two people just out of school. I knew I had to do something to protect us against misunderstandings about the love offerings."[52]

～

"I was horrified by the implication. Was I an Elmer Gantry who had successfully fleeced another flock? Many might just decide that I was."[53]

～

"So I went to Jesse Bader, who was then secretary of evangelism with the Federal Council of Churches. I said, 'Dr. Bader, I want your advice. How should we handle our finances?' He said, 'Billy you're going to have to do something that will take tremendous courage. But if you do it you could set an example for all evangelists in the years to come. Form a board of trustees, let them pay you a salary comparable to the salary of a large-church pastor, and then let the board handle the financing of all your crusades and expenses.' That's exactly what we did. I asked him to do one other thing: 'Will you and the council of churches' evangelism committee set my salary?' He said yes, and set my salary at $15,000 a year."[54]

～

Presents from admirers also became a problem. Grady Wilson said that in the early days, "about every town we'd go to, the car dealers would always furnish cars for us, the business folk would tell us, 'We'll look after you boys; don't worry about anything.'"

Gifts included, according to Graham, a new Buick from a local dealer, golf clubs, stereos, wardrobes from local haberdasheries, and ties from a local department store. One couple from Texas provided Graham with a new suit for each crusade. In 1970 he was named one of the year's best dressed men:

> *"I just don't know how it happened. Nearly all my clothes are given to me. I don't think I've bought a suit of clothes for four or five years. I did buy a sport coat once—a yellow coat—because the people on the TV want me to wear more colorful clothes."[55]*

NOTE: Graham finally established a "no personal gifts" rule, but made an exception when singer Johnny Cash sent him dozens of boxes filled with denim clothing.

⌒

The Internal Revenue Service soon required that the gifts be declared as income:

> *"I insist on being audited every year. I've instructed my lawyers not to dispute any gray areas . . . but I'm not accepting any gifts anymore. See this suit? I've slept in this suit, I guess about 20 times. I've had it about six or seven years."[56]*

⌒

In 1952 a wealthy man offered to underwrite Graham's work so he would never have to worry about finances. Graham responded, "I can't accept it. We get about three or four thousand letters a week and in most of those letters there'll be a dollar bill, sometimes $5, but every letter says, 'Billy, I'm praying for you.' My work would nose-dive immediately if people knew that a rich man was underwriting me."[57]

~

Most of the financial support for Graham's work comes from thousands of people who send small amounts to BGEA every month. BGEA is backed by no large foundations, advertising, product sales, or the like.

"Billy is honorable and open in the area of personal ethics," says T. W. Wilson, who was with BGEA for many years. "I have been with him when people have offered him homes, airplanes, and all kinds of other things. He has always responded, 'I cannot accept any personal gifts.' He wants no gray areas in his life—he is a man of integrity."[58]

~

"I was frightened—and I still am—that I would do something to dishonor the Lord."[59]

~

"If I had any advice to give to my brethren in parachurch organizations, it would be that they have total integrity, strict accountability, and public disclosure of finances. I think we see all these in the way Paul handled the money he collected for the Jerusalem church."[60]

~

In recent years Graham has received a salary of around $110,000 and has all of his expenses paid when doing crusade work. Both Billy and Ruth appreciate the ability to have raised their children and educated them well.

Considering that evangelists frequently preach that money is the root of all evil, Graham was asked if there were things he was glad he has the money to buy. He responded: "Yes, I'm glad that I can give my family a home, and I'm glad that I can give them good food. I'm glad that I can give them a good education and those things that I think all of us want for our families. And I think that I'm also glad that I was able to purchase a television set so we could watch the Beatles."[61]

∿

At the Lausanne Congress on World Evangelism in 1974, Ruth Graham refused to sign the Lausanne Covenant. She challenged the Reverend John Stott's insistence on the inclusion of the simple lifestyle clause, which read: "Those of us who live in affluent circumstances accept our duty to develop a simple lifestyle in order to contribute more generously to both relief and evangelism."

"If you had said 'simpler,'" Ruth said, "I would sign it. But what is '*simple*'? I have five kids."[62]

∿

In 1977 a Los Angeles television producer called for greater transparency for BGEA's financial status. The producer noted that 2 million people each year make contributions, which totaled between $15 million to $22 million even as far back as 1977. Although the television special made no claim that Graham misused the funds, it insisted that evangelic crusades should be covered by consumer laws so that people could know exactly where their money is going.[63]

During the 1970s the Knight-Ridder newspaper chain spent several years investigating the finances of the Billy Graham Evangelical Association but found no substantial irregularities.

~

Graham writes a monthly letter to contributors informing them of what he is doing and requesting their prayers. At the end of each letter he mentions the financial picture and asks for their help. Graham writes each of these letters himself—he does not hire professional fund-raising assistance. At Christmas, donors receive a Christmas card with a photograph of the entire Graham family.

BGEA uses the money from the crusades and from donations to finance a wide range of religious projects, including the funding of medical projects worldwide, a Bible study center at The Cove near Asheville, North Carolina, and an evangelism research center at Wheaton College near Chicago.

~

Throughout his life, money continued to fly in to Graham personally, from book royalties, along with

$250,000 from the sale of his father's land. Graham found himself with an embarrassment of riches.

His wife, Ruth, says, "Bill literally spends hours, *hours*, trying to figure out how not to make money. He has tried harder than anyone else I've ever known *not* to make money."[64]

"It's even occurred to me that I might give it all away someday and go off and live like Gandhi did."[65]

Graham once was asked why he didn't travel like Jesus did. Why would he sail to Europe on this big, beautiful, luxurious *Queen Mary*? Graham replied, "Well, Jesus traveled on a donkey; You find me a donkey that can swim the Atlantic, and I'll try to buy him."[66]

THE TOOLS OF EVANGELISM

Preaching the gospel is more difficult today than it was in years past:

"Because we have the competition today of the media, the magazines, and printed page and so forth that hold a different view, young and older people alike are tempted toward fraud, immorality, drugs . . . Those things were not a problem when I was a boy."[67]

Graham says he didn't think television would amount to much of anything when he first heard of it. But he had been successful in his radio ministry, and it didn't take long before he saw the benefits of television and other new technology:

> *"We used to reach hundreds, now we can reach thousands, even millions in one night across the world. We have had several nights and days in which we go into many languages, around 38 to 40 languages."*[68]

~

Billy Graham began to preach on the radio in 1943, his first year of ministry in Illinois. In his debut radio sermon, Graham got right to the point regarding conversion:

> *"The first thing we have to do is repent, the second to receive Christ, and the third to obey Christ. So it's repent, receive, obey."*[69]

~

Graham eventually expanded his crusade into all public communication media. In 1950 his group founded Worldwide Pictures to make religious films. One of its most charming, although amateurish, production was *Gospel Road—The Story of Jesus.* Filmed on location in Israel, the short movie starred Johnny Cash, John Denver, and Kris Kristopherson, singing songs written for the production by singer and songwriter Larry Gatlin. All of the musicians were very young.

~

When he started *Christianity Today* magazine in 1955, Graham envisioned a publication with hard-hitting editorials on current topics, full coverage of religious issues, biblical articles, book reviews, and a positive, broad-based approach. This viewpoint was to extend to "the great social issues of our day, such as the starving people in India, the racial problem, and others. We must be for the underdog and the downtrodden, as we all believe Christ was."[70]

~

Why start a magazine?

> *"There was a tremendous vacuum in religious publishing. The* Christian Century *was about the only Protestant magazine being quoted in the secular press. It had the field to itself, and it was considered quite liberal in those days. I had ideas about a magazine similar to* Christian Century, *one that would give theological respectability to evangelicals. . . . We were convinced that the magazine would be useless if it had the old, extreme fundamentalist stamp on it. (The word 'fundamentalist' at that time perhaps had a different, more negative connotation than it does today, on both sides of the Atlantic. I have always strongly accepted the fundamental doctrines of the faith and wanted the magazine to reflect this, but not to have a strong separatist or negative attitude.) It needed to avoid the extremes of both the right and the left. We felt that as much as possible editorials should present both sides of every issue and argument, but with an evangelical twist."[71]*

~

When the Internet became a popular means of mass communications, the Billy Graham Evangelistic Association was ready. BGEA set up a Web site (www.Billygraham. org) at which Internet surfers can read an invitation from Graham to make a commitment to Christ. One section of the Web page is called Steps to Peace With God. It consists of four steps, each offering excerpts from the Bible pertaining to the gospels. At the fourth step, the reader is invited to receive Christ into his or her life. The end of the fourth step reads: "If you have made a commitment to Christ, Billy Graham has a message to share with you. 'Go There.'" A mouse click takes the reader to a page entitled "Commitment to Christ. A Word from Billy Graham," which contains reassuring words and instructions to the just-converted reader:

"Here are some basic facts about this life. First, the Bible is food for the spiritual life, which needs to be nourished just as your body does. . . . Second, prayer is your lifeline to God. . . Third, a Christian is to be Christ's witness. You are to be an ambassador to Him wherever you go. . . . Fourth, you can't be an effective Christian on your own. If you are not already a member, get involved in a church where the Word of God is faithfully proclaimed."[72]

The reader is then offered a free six month subscription to *Decision Magazine* and is invited to call the BGEA Christian Guidance Department for any additional needs he or she may have. Readers who fill out a form with their name and address will receive Bible study materials, literature, and a free Billy Graham wall calendar.

∼

BILLY GRAHAM AND EARTHLY ISSUES

LIVING AS A CHRISTIAN

When asked if he believed there's a special kind of happiness enjoyed by believers, Graham responded: "Yes . . . a happiness the average person doesn't understand. It's just for those who know God. It's even in the sex experience."[1]

~

Time itself is a gift from God. Each of us, rich or poor, has 168 hours each week at our disposal, and once past, these hours can never be retrieved:

> *"Each human being has exactly the same number of hours and minutes each day. In Psalm 90 the Bible says that our allotted time on earth may be 70, or 80 years, or possibly a few more. The Psalmist goes on to say, 'Teach us to number our days aright so that we may gain a heart of wisdom.'"[2]*

~

> *"God calls us to invest our time, our very lives, primarily in people, not in projects or possessions."[3]*

On personal behavior:

"We are to be radiant. We should be chivalrous, courteous, clean of body, pure of mind, poised and gracious. We need to avoid silly flirtations, gossip, shady conversations, and suggestive amusements. We should be neat in appearance and dress with good taste. We should avoid extremes. Our lives and our appearance should commend the gospel and make it attractive to others."[4]

Graham on adversity:

"Comfort and prosperity have never enriched the world as much as adversity has done."[5]

Graham on humor:

"A keen sense of humor helps us to overlook the unbecoming, understand the unconventional, tolerate the unpleasant, overcome the unexpected, and outlast the unbearable."[6]

Graham on love:

"Love is never neutral. To preserve some things, it must destroy others. And that will inevitably stir opposition."[7]

Graham on sharing:

> *"Don't be content to have too much when millions in the world have too little. We need to remember every time we read the Bible that millions have no Bible to read. Let our lives, our means, and our prayers be shared with those millions who at this moment are wondering whether there is any relief from their distress."*[8]

~

> *"Let those of us who have the resources begin today to help [the homeless]. God has given us two hands— one to receive with and the other to give with. We are not cisterns made for hoarding, but are channels made for sharing."*[9]

~

Graham on grief:

> *"Many times grief is accompanied by guilt; whether real or false, guilt compounds grief."*[10]

~

Graham on humility:

> *"God measures people by the dimension of humility and not by the bigness of their achievements or the size of their capabilities."*[11]

~

MARRIAGE

"I believe that if you are a Christian, God has the ideal person picked out for you. If you don't wait for God's choice, you get his second or third best. I feel God picked out Ruth for me long before I met her, and he eventually revealed this to both of us."[12]

~

"I'll never forget one memorable hike with my three daughters. We were resting on a level place where we could look out over endless miles of hills and valleys, and somehow the question came up of how girls found the right boys to marry. So I told them that marriages were made in heaven and that God had already picked out a little boy for each of my little girls, and when they were all grown up, He would bring them together, and somehow they would know. And sitting close to one another and close to heaven, we all prayed for those three unknown little boys."[13]

~

"Many marriages end by the fifth year because couples haven't learned how to adjust. Differences can be settled amicably if both are really seeking the Lord's will. . . . A man especially needs to learn to be extremely gentle. A woman must have tenderness from her spouse; she can love him and respond to him if he is tender—no matter what he looks like or whether or not he is successful. We have found

that marriage should be made up of two forgivers.
We need to learn to say, 'I was wrong; I'm sorry.'
And we also need to say, 'That's all right, I love
you.'"[14]

~

Billy Graham often says that the Bible instructs us on how to love in I Corinthians, verses 3, 4 and 5. For the word charity, substitute the word love:

"And though I bestow all my goods to feed the poor, and though I give my body to be burned, and have not charity, it profiteth me nothing.

Charity suffereth long, and is kind; charity envieth not; charity vaunteth not itself, is not puffed up.

Doth not behave itself unseemingly, seeketh not her own, is not easily provoked, thinketh no evil" (The King James Bible).

~

Graham agreed with some of the goals of the women's movement, such as equal pay for equal work and women in the clergy. However, in 1978 he said that the changes in roles in the home threatens the Bible's prescription for a Christian home.

"The so-called emancipation of women causes young
women to postpone marriage and older women to
get out of it as soon as they can. The women's move-
ment is freeing the man from his responsibilities as
head of the home."[15]

~

Nevertheless, Graham was supportive to women in their efforts to live up to their full potential. "Daddy always believed in me, bragged on me, and encouraged me to follow my call to preach," said Anne Lotz. "It's the family blessing."[16]

PERSONAL MORALITY

"Those entrusted with leadership bear a special responsibility to uphold the highest standards of moral and ethical conduct, both publicly and privately. Those who have the greatest standing in society—whether clergy, politician, business person, labor leader, athlete, entertainer or anyone else who is a role model—also have the greatest need of personal integrity."[17]

~

"Concerning morals: I'm sure I've been tempted, especially in my younger years. But there has never been anything close to an incident. I took precautions. From the earliest days I've never had a meal alone with a woman other than Ruth, not even in a restaurant. I've never ridden in an automobile alone with a woman."[18]

~

In 1948, in Modesto, California, Graham gathered his small group in a hotel room to make an unusual pact.

To prevent sexual rumors, each man pledged never again to be alone with a woman other than his wife. The "Modesto Manifesto" also made a commitment to honest statistical reports and open finances.[19]

Graham knows that he is a target for those who would like to discredit him, and there have been near misses. The closest he's come to a risqué public scene was in London's Soho district:

> "This girl . . . was handed over the other people. I saw her coming and I said, 'Good night and God bless you,' and I jumped in the middle of some policemen. She was on drugs and . . . she was going to undress and have her picture taken because all the television cameras were there. She finally was able to get on top of our car, and as we left they had a picture of her on the top of the car and it was on the front page of every newspaper in Britain."[20]

> "There is always the chance of misunderstanding. I remember walking down the street in New York with my beautiful blond daughter, Bunny. I was holding her hand. I heard somebody behind us say, 'There goes Billy Graham with one of those blond girls.'"[21]

> "On one of our crusades to Germany, Bev Shea [one of Graham's assistants, who despite his name, is a

103

male], Cliff Barrows, and I went out to eat at a restaurant. The next day the papers reported that 'Billy Graham ate at a restaurant last evening in the company of a woman named Beverley Shea.'"[22]

~

Even though Graham says he saw shocking sexual behavior in London's parks, he was unwilling to condemn all of England. In fact:

"I think the British people have a higher standard of morals than the entire western world."[23]

~

During an unofficial visit to Moscow in the 1950s, Graham noted:

"In the Moscow parks, I saw thousands of young people but I did not see one locked in an embrace. I hate Communism, but I love the Russian people and the moral purity I found among the Muscovites."[24]

~

"Let me make clear that sex is not a sin. Sex is a gift from God, but if it is misused, it is frightening. It causes death and judgment and hell."[25]

~

In 1993, in a sermon to 44,000 people, Graham said:

"Is AIDS a judgment from God? I cannot say for sure, but I think so."

Two weeks later he said, "To say God has judged people with AIDS would be very wrong and very cruel, I would like to say that I am very sorry for what I said."[26]

Later he told the *Cleveland Plain Dealer*:"I don't believe that, and I don't know why I said it."[27]

~

Graham once devoted most of a Denver, Colorado, crusade to speaking out on AIDS prevention.

"God loves homosexuals as much as anyone else. I think homosexuality is a sin, but no greater than idolatry or adultery."[28]

~

Graham issued a press release acknowledging that his recent reference to the castration of rapists was "an offhand, hasty, spontaneous remark at a news conference that I regretted almost as soon as I said it."

In a follow-up release Graham said, "I meant to come back to it [the remark that castration would stop the rapist 'pretty quick'] before the conference was over and correct it, but I got sidetracked on other issues." He added, "It is interesting that the thought of castration for some people stirs a far more violent reaction than the idea of rape itself. Perhaps this is a part of our permissive society's sickness."[29]

~

On being asked by TV interviewer Larry King if he ever lied publicly, Graham responded: "No, not that

I can recall. But I'm not going to say never, never, never."[30]

RAISING CHILDREN

In regard to children, Graham stresses the importance of kindness and praise:

> *"We add to the hurt when we are critical. Criticism has a withering effect upon people, especially our children. They need guidance and correcting, but constant criticism will destroy their spirit and their ability to succeed."*[31]

∽

> *"We flourish with kindness and shrivel with unkindness."*[32]

∽

When Graham was a youngster and even as he was raising his own family, spanking was the accepted form of discipline. But it is not the most effective way of teaching, says Graham.

> *"Children are more impressed by the conduct of others than by lectures or spanking."*[33]

∽

> *"The entertainment world has influenced the family in a dangerous direction, I truly believe that."*[34]

∽

"Many young people today have unrealistic expectations because they live in an unreal world that has been created by movies and television. If they see a complicated situation on television or in a film, the problem is solved within 20 or 30 minutes. Then when they encounter that same kind of problem they think it ought to be solved immediately; yet it may take years. We expect it to be instant. We think that we can have instant gratification and instant everything." [35]

"TV could have a great moral impact if it could devise the ways." [36]

"If we love the young people of America, we will do everything in our power to destroy things that hurt their character and jeopardize their future, things such as drugs and pornography." [37]

In 1972, at a time when the anti-Vietnam war movement was raging and the sexual revolution was in full force, Graham wrote in an article for the *Saturday Evening Post*:

"The vast majority of American young people are still alienated, uncommitted, and uninvolved. There is a deep vacuum within them. They are searching for individual identity. They are searching for a

challenge and a faith. Whoever captures the imagination of the youth of our generation will change the world. Youth movements of the past have been perverted and led by dictators and demagogues. Perhaps the American young people will be captured by Jesus Christ.

~

Later in the article Graham wrote to young people:

"I see that you are impatient. I see that you are angry, and I say that you will have your chance to change the world. I say that you can succeed in your dreams. I pray that you will succeed as no other generation in history has succeeded for several reasons:

"Because you have a better education.

"Because you are brighter than earlier generations.

"Because you are healthier and will live longer.

"Because you and your friends, by the thousands, are discovering Jesus Christ."[38]

NOTE: A person who was 21 years old when Graham wrote these words would be 48 years old in 1999.

~

Although Graham believes in a Christian upbringing, he does not advocate forcing religion upon a child:

"The very nature of true religion is that it is voluntary. Every person must make his own free choice when all the information is in his possession."[39]

GROWING UP IN THE GRAHAM HOUSEHOLD

Billy and Ruth Graham have five children, now all grown. Franklin, who heads up a worldwide medical missionary movement, is the oldest son. A tall man who looks much like his father, Franklin is expected to take over the crusades when Billy dies. The Grahams have three daughters, Anne, Virginia (called Gigi), and Ruth (called Bunny), and a second son, Ned. All of the Graham children work in the Christian ministry.

Bunny Graham Dienert says of her father, "I don't connect Daddy with Billy Graham. To me they are two different people. Daddy is just Daddy and I don't share him with the world. When he's being Billy Graham, that's different."[40]

～

Graham's prolonged crusades in distant cities sometimes put a strain on the family. Graham recalls one night when he returned home from a long trip and found his toddler son, Franklin, sleeping in his mother's room. Franklin awoke and asked his mother, "Who him?"[41]

～

It was a sad moment for Graham when his daughter, Gigi, took him to task: "I had been very rude, and he spanked me. I asked him in anger what kind of father he thought he was anyway, always being gone. Tears filled his eyes. . . . Now as a parent, I understand quite fully the anguish he must have gone through at times, wondering if he was making the right decision by leaving."[42]

～

Gigi Graham said that as a teenager, her favorite newspaper comic was Dennis the Menace because it reminded her of her little brother Franklin.

Betty Frist, a neighbor of the Grahams in Montreat, recounts a story about Franklin Graham when he was very young. Billy and Franklin were sitting together in church when the offering plate was passed. Franklin confidently dipped into the plate, putting in a coin and taking one out. Graham looked shocked and grabbed his son's hand and held it in a viselike grip. Franklin was bewildered and indignant. "I'm makin' *change*," he told his dad. Apparently the little boy had put in a nickel and taken out a quarter.[43]

～

Graham's daughter, Bunny, recalls hiding with her sister behind trees and throwing mudpies at cars, and allowing sightseers to take her picture for a nickel a time—until their mother found out and stopped them.

Discipline was firm in the Graham household, explained Bunny. Rules were carefully spelled out and, if they were broken, punishment followed swiftly. "Daddy didn't like to deny us anything when he was home, but when he said jump we jumped. I can remember his whipping me three times, though. Once, because I told mother I hated her; another time when I kicked my brother in the head; and the third, when I told a lie and wouldn't retract it. Daddy always punished first and explained later. But after it was all over, we'd pray together for guidance. And he'd put his arms around us and tell us he loved us."[44]

∼

Graham wanted to be sure his children learned the facts of life, so he suggested to Ruth that they raise animals on their property so that they could learn about sex and reproduction naturally by observing. The practical Ruth said, "Why not just *tell* them and save ourselves all that trouble?"[45]

Nevertheless, Little Piney Cove was home to many dogs and other pets.

∼

Franklin also remembers an incident where an emotionally disturbed man showed up at the Grahams' home. Billy answered the door while Franklin watched through a side window. Franklin says he couldn't hear the conversation, but suddenly his father slugged the man, who immediately fell to the ground.

"When the man began to cry, Daddy knelt beside him and talked for a while. Then Daddy prayed with him, helped him to his feet, and sent him on his way. He never bothered us again."

"I knew Daddy was strong and wasn't to be pushed around. He had come off the farm and was as tough as an old ax handle."[46]

~

Franklin loved camping with his father. They would climb the ridge behind Little Piney Cove and set up camp. As they roasted marshmallows over the hot coals, Graham enthralled Franklin with tales of Granddaddy Graham and about his own boyhood days on the farm.

They laid their bedrolls close to the fire, but Billy had placed his bedroll on a slope. In the morning Franklin woke up, and looked for his father: "He was gone! I jumped up and looked around, my heart pounding. Where was he? Then I saw his sleeping bag about 25 yards away next to a fallen log. I ran to the bag and bent over. He was in it. To my amazement he was still fast asleep—completely unaware that he had been on quite a journey during the night. If it hadn't been for that log, he may have rolled all the way to the bottom of the mountain."[47]

~

Graham, who became depressed when there were too many dark or rainy days, began talking of leaving North Carolina after a trip to Europe in 1960. Ruth, whose parents lived in nearby Montreat, always put a stop to such notions.

"Only a few months had passed after our return from Europe." recalled Franklin, "when Daddy began talking about spending the winter of 1960–1961 in Vero Beach, Florida. I knew Daddy was thinking seriously about moving to Florida. He loved the warm, sunny weather.

"After we arrived in Vero Beach, Daddy spoke enthusiastically about moving us there permanently. Once again, though, Mama stepped in and settled the topic for good. 'Bill, if you're going to travel, I'm going to live near my parents. I'm going to need their help in raising this family.'"[48]

∿

Ruth Graham has definite convictions. When asked if she believed in women's liberation, she said with her eyes twinkling: "Yes, I believe that women should be liberated from all outside work so they can stay home and take care of their children."[49]

∿

Ned Graham was a gentle boy, but by his own admission Franklin was a restless spirit. Both men had turbulent teen years. "Just because my father was Billy Graham," said Franklin, "I wasn't going to live the life everybody expected me to live."[50]

∿

Franklin Graham started smoking early, liked fast cars, motorcycles and airplanes, and often was in trouble at school. Anne Graham Lotz says she was well into adulthood and experiencing trouble with her own marraige before she realized what her mother's situation had been.

"As a girl, I loved the Lord and I loved His Word. When I drifted from Him, I looked back and I could see my mother raising the five of us without a husband present in the home everyday. And I never saw her lose her temper, just completely come unglued. After being with Franklin all day, you could have had the tendency to lose your temper."[51]

$\sim$

Franklin once told a group, "If my mom has white hair, it's because of me!" To which Ruth Graham replied, "Don't take all the credit son. Age has something to do with it."

Then Ruth added, "With age has come the ever-growing, ever-deepening awareness of the relevance and the assurance of God's promise. Not one has failed! When folks say, 'You must be proud of Franklin,' we realized that it is not a matter of pride, but of gratitude to God for his faithfulness. With God, nobody's hopeless."[52]

$\sim$

Franklin Graham says that he had to come to God in his own way: "People might say 'come on, you've got it made. You've got a perfect position before God.' No, I don't. No one can choose God for you. You must choose."[53]

Franklin made his personal commitment to Christ and to preaching the gospel in a hotel room near Jerusalem when he was 22 years old.

∽

As Billy Graham's fame grew, it became difficult for the family to bid good-bye to him in public, where he was swamped by fans and autograph seekers. Once his daughter Anne accompanied him to the airport and was immediately swept into the background by a crowd of well-wishers. Rapidly shaking one hand after another, Graham turned to his daughter, who was shyly standing behind him. Grasping her hand, he blurted, "Nice to meet you," before dashing to his plane.[54]

∽

"My father, away from home so much of the time, left most of the responsibilities and burdens of rearing five children to my mother. . . when he was home, he led us in daily Bible reading and prayer. How precious it was to have him take his role as a spiritual leader seriously. He practiced at home what he preached in public. Children need to see fathers on their knees, acknowledging and bowing to a higher authority, and loving their mother."[55]

∽

FAMILY PLANNING

Billy Graham seems to see complexity in the issues of overpopulation, birth control, and abortion.

"The world now faces a biological problem as well as a political one. Are we capable of mustering the will, the wisdom, and the compassion to cope with this mounting problem of overpopulation? No present or future schemes of socialistic or altruistic welfare to share the wealth can mean much if there are more people than there is wealth to be shared. Thus people themselves have become a weapon which could ultimately destroy them. Sexual energy is one of the flames out of control."[56]

∽

"I am a strong advocate of birth control. I know this runs contrary to some Catholic doctrine but I suspect that many Catholics practice it.

"I'm not in favor of abortion, except where there is rape, incest, or where the mother's life is in jeopardy."[57]

∽

"Few issues have polarized our society as much as the debate over abortion. There admittedly are isolated cases where abortion is the lesser of two evils, such as when the mother's life is clearly at risk. However, for many people today abortion has become little more than another means of birth control, practiced for mere personal convenience with

no regard for the fate of the infant growing in the womb. When Mary, the virgin mother of Jesus, visited her cousin, Elizabeth, who was pregnant with John the Baptist, we are told that Elizabeth declared to Mary, 'As soon as the sound of your greeting reached my ears, the baby in my womb leaped for joy' (Luke 1:44). This is a clear indication that that unborn infant was a person, not just a piece of tissue."[58]

~

Graham expressed his dismay over President Bill Clinton's 1996 veto of legislation criminalizing so-called partial-birth abortions: "I think the President was wrong in vetoing it. I had the opportunity of telling him that in person."[59]

~

On the other hand, Graham has been critical of anti-abortion activists such as "Operation Rescue."

"I think they have gone much too far, and their cause has been hurt. The tactics ought to be prayer and discussion."[60]

~

On being asked to comment on the killing of an abortion doctor in Massachusetts, Graham said: "I think it was absolutely terrible and hideous, and it shows the depth of man's heart and evil that would do something like that."[61]

Graham suggests that the moral dilemmas that face us at the beginning of life may also present themselves at the end of life:

"There has always been a 'time to live and a time to die.' Today, with the ability to prolong life, each one of us will probably have to face this issue ourselves or with someone we love. . . . How long is too long?"[62]

SCIENCE AND TECHNOLOGY

"Young people of today have lived through a technological revolution. But also they see degeneration on television, they see an emphasis on sex and violence in our entertainment."[63]

"Our Western civilization may die with all of its political, economic, social, and scientific achievements. Indeed, the latter may be the cause of its death. This is the generation that produced DDT to kill bugs, 2-4-D to kill weeds, formula 1080 to kill rats, and the E=MC squared to wipe out populations."[64]

On whether science can overtake belief:

"No, billions and billions of stars and planets out there, and behind them all is God."[65]

With all the alienation from self that science and technology can bring, it also brings new ideas for Graham's sermons:

"I read an article about the great Beijing-to-Paris car race that was first run in 1907. Today it's still one of the longest and most grueling automobile races in the world. That route now covers 16,000 kilometers across 2 continents, 11 countries, 3 deserts, and too many rivers to count. When the race was first run, finding the way was the major problem. Today each car is equipped with a global positioning system, an electronic device that sends a signal to a satellite. It shows the driver and the navigator their position on a computerized map.

"But even with this high-tech navigational help, the basic challenge of the race remains the same. One navigator said, 'We'll always know where we are, but the problem is, where should *we be?' That seems to summarize a great deal of the tension in our world today. In our countries, in our homes, in our families, and deep within our hearts we may know where we are. The problem is where* should *we be."[66]*

RACIAL DISCRIMINATION

Over the years, Billy Graham's life is a story of public and visible growth and development, both intellectual and spiritual. Nowhere is this more evident than the changes in his thinking about racial issues. When

Graham was a teen, there was a black barbershop in downtown Charlotte which gave great haircuts, cheap. Many of Billy's friends started going there. Billy would not:

"Long as there's a white barbershop in Charlotte, I'll never have my hair cut at a nigger barbershop. Never."[67]

～

In the early years of his ministry Graham and a visiting British evangelist got into an intense discussion over an incident when their driver, a black man, was forced to buy food at the back door of a café. Graham is said to have told the British evangelist: "If it weren't for you wretched Britishers, we wouldn't have any Negroes in this country; we wouldn't have this mess."[68]

～

At one point in those early years, Graham said: "Only when Christ comes again will the little white children walk hand in hand with the little black children."[69]

～

Over time, Graham's racial views shifted:

"It rarely occurred to me in my childhood to think about the difficulties, problems, and oppressions of black people. In high school, I began to question some of the practices, but it was not until I'd actually committed my life to Christ that I began to think more deeply about it."[70]

~

Wheaton College, Graham's alma mater, was founded as an anti-slavery school and, according to Graham, remained "very strong in its social conscience, especially on the race question. I began to realize for the first time that if I were a Christian, I had to take a stand."[71]

~

In 1952 Graham began to speak out against segregation and prejudice in the church.

"Of all people, Christians should be the most active in reaching out to those of other races."[72]

~

Graham refused to accept a speaking engagement unless all people could sit where they wished:

"That was among my first acts of conscience on the race question. I determined from then on I would never preach to another segregated audience."[73]

~

The change for Graham took time. Early on, he objected to strict enforcement of Supreme Court antidiscrimination rulings.

"I am convinced that forced integration will never work. You cannot make two races love each other and accept each other at the point of bayonets. It must come from the heart if it is to be successful."[74]

~

Like many southerners, Graham felt that his region of the country took an unfair amount of blame for racial problems. He believed that the South was moving faster toward a climate of tolerance:

> *"I see very little possibility of the North solving its racial problems. The blacks and the whites do not know each other. In the South they know each other. When the servant-master relationship is finished in the next generation I think the South will have pretty well solved its racial problem and is headed that way very fast right now. I think Mr. Carter's emergence [as president] is indicative of that, with the black support of a peanut farmer from Georgia."[75]*

Events, however, pushed Graham to take an even stronger stand against racial discrimination. When Arkansas governor Orval Faubus ordered the National Guard to Little Rock in 1957 to resist the Supreme Court's school desegregation order, President Eisenhower called Graham to tell him he was thinking of sending in federal troops.

Graham responded, "Mr. President, I think that is the only thing you can do. It is out of hand, and the time has come to stop it."[76]

That afternoon 1,000 troops of the 101st Airborne Division rolled into Little Rock. Later Graham journeyed to Little Rock on a healing mission. He talked and prayed with prisoners who had bombed various buildings. Integrationist pastor W. O. Vaught told

Graham that "there has been universal agreement in all the churches and out across the city that your visit here was one of the finest."[77]

～

After his 1960 African crusade Graham said, "They [Africans] could not see American Christianity as the model for the oneness of the body of Christ. How could they think otherwise when they heard that a person of color was barred from entering certain churches in the United States? I came away more determined than ever to do what I could as an evangelist to combat the grim legacy of racism in my own country."[78]

～

Racial prejudice, Graham says, is a sin because it violates God's law to love our neighbor and because it has its roots in pride and arrogance:

"Racism is not only a social problem . . . because racism is a sin, it is also a moral and spiritual issue. Legal and social efforts to obliterate racism (or at least curb its more onerous effects) have a legitimate place. However, only the supernatural love of God can change our hearts in a lasting way and replace hatred and indifference with love and active compassion."[79]

～

In the early 1960s, Graham was asked if it were not true that there were no black people on Noah's Ark or at the

Last Supper. Graham warned not to make assumptions based on the Bible's silence:

> *"Simply because the Bible does not mention whether or not negroes were involved in either of these occasions, does not prove either way. It only indicates that in the scriptures no issue has been made of the racial differences. The differences are superficial at best, and if anything is true in the Word of God, it is the truth expressed in 1 Samuel 16:7, where it is written 'For man looketh on the outward appearance, but the Lord looketh on the heart.'"*[80]

~

> *"There may be reasons that men give for practicing racial discrimination, but let's not make the mistake of pleading the Bible to defend it."*[81]

~

In 1960 Graham wrote:

> *"Many of those, especially in South Africa, who believe in racial superiority quote the Bible. How they can twist and distort the Scriptures to support racial superiority is beyond me. Most of them quote the passage from the last part of the ninth chapter of Genesis, where it is recorded that Noah cursed Canaan and his children to be servants. There is no proof that Canaan was ever dark skinned, and it is most certainly debatable."*[82]

~

"It is true that God called Israel to be unique among the nations and told them to separate themselves from the evil nations round about them. But the white race cannot possibly claim to be the chosen race nor can the white race take for themselves promises that were applied to ancient Israel."[83]

～

"It seems to me . . . that the whole weight of Scripture is for treating all men with neighbor-love, regardless of race or color."[84]

～

"It must be remembered that 70 percent of the world's population is colored. They are growing in power, strength, and numbers."[85]

～

By 1994 Graham stood firmly for ending all forms of racial prejudice:

"Integration is the only solution. We've got to be totally integrated—in our homes, in our worship services, even in marriage."[86]

～

"Any man who has a genuine conversion experience will find his racial attitudes greatly changed."[87]

～

". . . if you preach the love of Christ and the transforming power of Christ, there is not only a spiritual change but a psychological and moral change. The

man who receives Christ forgets all about race when he is giving his life to Christ."[88]

~

"When it comes to the church, there is the Chinese church, the Korean church, the white churches, the Negro churches, etc. Why? The reason is that the church is probably the most voluntary of all organizations. There is nothing sinful in races wanting to stay together. The sin comes when a church puts up its color bar at the Cross of Christ."[89]

~

Graham tells a story that supposedly occurred just after the end of the Civil War:

"A Negro entered a fashionable church in Richmond, Virginia, one Sunday morning while communion was being served. He walked down the aisle and knelt at the altar. A rustle of shock and anger swept through the congregation. Sensing the situation, a distinguished layman immediately stood up, stepped forward to the altar and knelt beside his colored brother. Captured by his spirit, the congregation followed this magnanimous example.

"The layman who set the example was Robert E. Lee."[90]

~

RELIGIOUS TOLERANCE

In 1948 Graham said, "The three greatest menaces faced by orthodox Christianity are Communism, Roman Catholicism, and Mohammedanism."[91]

~

By 1960 Graham had softened his stand and was trying to build a bridge between the various religious philosophies:

> *"Ten years ago my concept of the church tended to be narrow and provincial, but after a decade of intimate contact with Christians the world over I am now aware that the family of God contains people of various ethnological, cultural, class, and denominational differences."[92]*

~

> *"I am far more tolerant of other kinds of Christians than I once was. My contact with Catholic, Lutheran and other leaders—people* far *removed from my Southern Baptist tradition—has helped me, hopefully, to move in the right direction. I've found that my beliefs are essentially the same as those of orthodox Roman Catholics, for instance. They believe in the Virgin Birth, and so do I. They believe in the blood atonement of the cross, and so do I. We only differ on some matters of later church tradition."[93]*

~

"The ecumenical movement has broadened my viewpoint and I recognize now that God has his people in all churches."[94]

~

When Graham attended meetings of the World Council of Churches (WCC), he said he was "thrilled at the whole process of seeing world churchmen sitting down together, praying together, discussing together."[95]

~

In 1966 Graham observed, "I find myself closer to Catholics than the radical Protestants. I think the Roman Catholic Church today is going through a second Reformation."[96]

~

When he was asked to endorse candidate John Kennedy in his 1960 campaign against Richard Nixon, Graham declined, largely because he wanted to stay out of politics, but he worried that this might be interpreted as an anti-Catholic position.

"In Kennedy's hometown of Boston, I had enjoyed good rapport with Cardinal Richard J. Cushing for 10 years, and I felt sincerely that it was important in our crusades to foster good church relationships. I did not agree with some Catholic teachings and church practices, but warm acquaintance and fellowship with many in that church had long since laid to rest whatever prejudices I might have had."[97]

~

In 1967 Graham said, "[This is] a time when Protestants and Catholics could meet together and greet each other as brothers, whereas 10 years ago they could not."[98]

~

On November 21, 1967, the Catholic priests who run Belmont Abbey College in North Carolina, conferred an honorary degree on Graham. In response, Graham said he "knew of no greater honor a North Carolina preacher, reared just a few miles from here, could have than to be presented with this degree. I'm not sure but what this could start me being called 'Father Graham.'"[99]

~

Graham was the first Protestant to speak at a vesper service at the Vatican's North American College. In 1972 he received the Catholic International Franciscan Award for "his contribution to true ecumenism."[100] Graham said, "While I am not worthy to touch the shoelaces of St. Francis, yet this same Christ that called Francis in the 13th century also called me to be one of his servants in the 20th century."[101]

~

During a visit to Israel in 1960, Graham expressed a philosophy that would become his hallmark—that people of all beliefs should be treated with respect:

"I want to thank you for proselytizing me, a Gentile, who has committed his life to a Jew who was born in this country and reared up here in Nazareth. I want to thank you for being the nation through whom Jesus was brought to this earth in the divine plan of God. And I want to thank you as one who has given my life to a Jew who, as a man living upon this earth, claimed to be God."[102]

∽

"I would never go after someone just because he is Jew, which is why I have never supported the Jewish Missions."[103]

∽

On a trip to Asia, Graham noted: "In the hotel room I am staying in they have a book: *The Teaching of Buddha*. And almost every day I have been here, I have read some of the sayings of Buddha. And many of those sayings are almost identical with the sayings of Jesus. There will be many things that we can identify with in other religions. [But] there is an exclusiveness to Christ. The devil is busy. There is a supernatural power of evil oppressing much of the world."[104]

∽

"It would not be easy to follow all the sayings of Buddha or live the kind of life Confucius would have us to live. To follow Jesus may be difficult, but compared to the others it's very easy, because Christ lives in our hearts, and he was raised from the dead."[105]

～

Graham once said that Mao Tse-Tung's "eight precepts are basically the same as the Ten Commandments."[106]

～

Christian extremists have censured Graham for his association with nonfundamentalist Christians and non-Christians alike.

> *"I have been called 'liberal' in some areas because of my stand on certain social issues; I have been called 'conservative' theologically. I accept both labels, and believe that I stand in the mainstream of evangelism."[107]*

～

> *"When our Lord spoke through John to the seven churches of Asia, he rebuked them for their sins, but he did not tell them all to join the same church— that wasn't one of their failings. I have no problems working with anyone, under any label, as long as he knows the Lord Jesus Christ as his Savior and is living the life of a Christian disciple."[108]*

～

> *"At the moment, I can go out and preach to labor leaders, business leaders, Catholics, Protestants, Jews, and they all accept me as a preacher of the gospel and I feel that this is my calling."[109]*

NOTE: For more about criticism of Graham for his religious tolerance, see the section "The Fundamentalists."

THE POPES

Upon the death of Pope John XXIII in 1963, Graham said, "I admired Pope John tremendously. . . . I felt he brought a new era to the world. It is my hope that the Cardinals elect a new Pope who will follow the same line as John. It would be a great tragedy if they chose a man who reacted against John."[110]

∽

"Since his election, Pope John Paul II has emerged as the greatest religious leader of the modern world, and one of the greatest moral and spiritual leaders of this century. . . . The Pope came [to America] as a statesman and a pastor, but I believe he also sees himself coming as an evangelist. . . . The Pope sought to speak to the spiritual hunger of our age in the same way Christians throughout the centuries have spoken to the spiritual yearnings of every age—by pointing people to Christ."[111]

∽

"The visit of Pope John Paul II to the United States [in 1979] is an event of great significance not only for Roman Catholics, but for all Americans—as well as the world . . . In the short time he has been the Pope, John Paul has become the moral leader of the world. My prayers and the prayers of countless other Protestants will be with him as he makes his journey."[112]

∽

Graham met Pope John Paul II in 1981 and their conversation lasted two hours. Their talk was "very private, [an] intimate conversation. He [the Pope] was extremely warm and interested in our work."[113]

~

"We discussed the Christian faith, both our agreements and some of our differences. I have great admiration for the Pope's moral courage, and sent him a cable as soon as I heard he had been shot to assure him of my prayers for his recovery."[114]

~

"I think the American people are looking for a leader, a moral and spiritual leader that believes something. And the Pope does. . . . Thank God, I've got somebody to quote now with some real authority."[115]

~

About a month after the Pope had visited Vancouver, Graham said of the Pope's message: "I'll tell you, that was just about as straight an evangelical address as I've ever heard. It was tremendous. Of course, I'm a great admirer of his. He gives moral guidance in a world that seems to have lost its way."[116]

~

Graham recalled his 1989 meeting with the Pope.

"There was a pause in the conversation; suddenly the Pope's arm shot out and he grabbed the lapels of

my coat, he pulled me forward within inches of his own face. He fixed his eyes on me and said, 'Listen, Graham, we are brothers.'"[117]

~ ✸ ~

NORTHERN IRELAND

In 1972 Billy Graham walked the notoriously violent Shankill and Falls roads in Belfast, Northern Ireland. As he stopped in to a Catholic pub, a loud explosion was heard nearby. Local residents asked the evangelist to give last rites to several Irish Republican Army (IRA) members and innocent bystanders, who were mortally wounded when a bomb terrorists were preparing ignited and exploded prematurely. Graham knelt beside the wounded and prayed for them.

Later Graham met privately with Cardinal Conway, the Roman Catholic primate of Ireland, at the archbishop's palace in Armagh. A Catholic priest Graham had met in Northern Ireland related how he had come to Christ through reading Graham's book, *Peace with God.*[118]

~

While Graham preached at a Protestant church at Ravenhill, Belfast, the Reverend Ian Paisley, the extremist Protestant minister, struck out at Graham from his own pulpit. "The church which has Billy Graham in its pulpit will have the curse of the Almighty on it," Paisley claimed.

Paisley said he turned down an invitation to lunch with Graham in London because he would not have fellowship with "those who deny the faith."[119]

~

"The Billy Graham Organization is a lying organization," charged Paisley. "It tells absolute lies. If it knows you are a Fundamentalist it will write you a letter and say, 'Billy Graham is a Fundamentalist and has nothing to do with the Church of Rome."[120]

~

Paisley, who has limited support with the Northern Ireland Protestant community, frequently condemns Irish Catholics, the Catholic Church, and the Pope as anti-Christ blasphemers. He painted Graham with the same brush:

> I tell you that if an angel from heaven appeared at the City Hall and preached another gospel, this city [Belfast] would turn almost entirely to that angel. Do you know that? Billy Graham comes as an angel of light, and people say, "Is he not so gracious? Is he not so kind? Is he not a lovely man?" *Satan can be transformed into an angel of light.* And no marvel, for Satan himself is transformed into an angel of light. Therefore it is no great thing if his ministers also be transformed as the ministers of righteousness, whose end shall be according to their works."[121]

~ ❋ ~

GRAHAM'S LIFE IN POLITICS

PATRIOTISM

Bill Moyers, a television personality, Baptist preacher, and President Lyndon Johnson's press aide, said, "Billy Graham represents a basic kind of patriotism in this country—an unquestioning, obeying patriotism, a loyalty to the authority of the president. Billy was always uncritical, unchallenging, unquestioning."[1]

Nevertheless, Graham has, over the years, modified his views of what it means to be an American:

"I preached Americanism too much. I used to think of America as symbolic of the kingdom of God. . . . The real kingdom is the kingdom of believers."[2]

"America is not a Christian country. It's a secular country in which many Christians dwell."[3]

Graham also seemed to feel that the capitalistic philosophy had been stretched a little too far in the United States:

"The great flaw in the American economic system for the past four decades has been an unrealistic faith in the power of prosperity rather than in the ultimate power and benevolence of God."[4]

AVOIDING POLITICS

In 1949 Billy Graham appeared before a joint session of the Georgia legislature to urge an old-fashioned revival of Temperance laws. Within two hours, by a healthy 34 to 5 vote the Senate had passed a bill to make the state bone dry. By the next day legislative ardor had cooled somewhat. Graham had rejected an invitation to "heat up" the House of Representatives as well. There the "bone-dry" bill rested in a pigeonhole in the Temperance Committee when the legislative session closed. Many a Georgia "wet'" lifted his thanksgiving glass, at so close a call.[5]

∽

Graham, at one time, also expressed his opinion on economics:

"We are going to spend ourselves into a depression. We can't keep on taking care of the whole world. But don't anybody tell Mr. Truman I said so."[6]

∽

Eventually, however, Graham decided to do his best to steer clear of politics:

> *"I don't want to get into any kind of politics, left or right, Republican or Democrat, because I experienced that a few times in my years, and you can get in trouble real fast."*[7]

~

Both at home and abroad, the public expected Graham to take stands on important issues. For example, when Graham visited Ghana in 1960, newspapers there berated him for not condemning the French government's plan to explode a nuclear device in the Sahara. The official paper of Prime Minister Kuame Nkrumah's Convention People's Party, the *Ghana Times*, said: "Not a few have been disappointed, actually stunned by Dr. Graham's attitude to the intention of Christian France to detonate an atom bomb in the Sahara, the evil effects of which will not spare any African Christians.

"To preach love and refuse to comment on the proposed act of a Christian nation which is the very reverse or negation of love is a matter that staggers the imagination," wrote the *Ghana Times*.

Back home, the *Asheville Citizen* carried the headline "Attendance Falls after Papers Hit Graham's Reticence on Bomb."[8]

~

On the political activism of the extreme religious right, Graham says: "I can identify with them on theology, probably, in many areas, but in the political emphases

138

they have, I don't, because I don't think Jesus or the Apostles took sides in the political arenas of their day."[9]

~

Presidents often called for Graham when they found themselves with a political controversy and felt that their position would be strengthened if it appeared to have the backing of a popular Christian leader:

"I've had three presidents offer me jobs, top positions, and I have said no to all of them—I don't know how many President Johnson has asked me to serve in."[10]

~

At a White House dinner not long before he left office, Johnson asked Billy Graham's opinion on a controversial political issue. Graham started to speak when Ruth gave him a kick under the table. Surprised, he glanced at her and began to speak again. She kicked him again.

"Ruth, why are you kicking me?" Graham asked.

"Because it's none of your business, Bill," she said.

"That's just what I was going to say," said Billy.

When dinner was over, the President said to Mrs. Graham, "You were right, Ruth. I shouldn't have asked that question."[11]

~

Apparently Dallas oil billionaire H. L. Hunt offered Billy Graham $6 million if he would run against Lyndon Johnson for the presidency in 1964. According to

Grady Wilson, Graham's close friend and assistant, the oil tycoon reached the evangelist one night at the Shamrock Hotel in Houston, informing him that the money would be deposited in his personal bank account if he allowed his name to be put in nomination at the Republican convention that summer. According to witnesses, Graham took no more than 15 seconds to tell Hunt that although he was flattered, he had no interest in relinquishing a post he considered more important than the presidency.[12]

~

The *Saturday Evening Post* asked Graham what he thought of suggestions that he would make a good president:

"Well, first of all, I couldn't get elected because people who come to hear me preach would immediately say, 'What is he doing in politics?'"[13]

~

Richard Nixon liked to say that when Graham went into the ministry, politics lost one of its greatest practitioners. Once he offered Graham the ambassadorship to Israel at a meeting with Golda Meir. Graham recalls: "I said the Mideast would blow up if I went over there."

When Graham declined, he recalls:

"Golda Meir reached under the table and squeezed my hand. She was greatly relieved."[14]

~

Graham considered Richard Nixon a special friend; even though he was shocked by the president's behavior in the Watergate scandal, he stood by Nixon as a friend. On one occasion Graham's loyalty to Nixon nearly disrupted a crusade service.

In 1970 Richard and Pat Nixon joined Billy and Ruth Graham at the Volunteer Stadium at the University of Tennessee in Knoxville. While many of those present gave a rousing welcome to Nixon and waved American flags, tension among the students hung thick in the air as Nixon rose to speak. By the time he was done, the mood had turned ugly, and the antiwar activists became quite vocal. The beloved gospel singer Ethel Waters rose to sing. With her trademark dazzling smile and kindly voice, she settled the crowd. "Now, children," she chided, "let mama sing."

The antiwar activists may not have been persuaded by the title of her song, "When You Know Him You Will Love Him," but apparently they accepted that Waters was singing about Jesus, not about Richard Nixon. They settled down and Graham was able to deliver his sermon.[15]

NOTE: For more about Graham's relationship with Nixon and his attempts to avoid political positions, see the section "The Presidents."

COMMUNISM

Graham wrote about communism in his autobiography, *Just As I Am*: "We are dealing with a treacherous and vicious enemy who has the supernatural forces of evil behind him."[16]

~

Graham was a fervent anti-Communist in the 1950s and went so far as to thank God for Senator Joseph McCarthy and the House Un-American Activities Committee, "who, in the face of public denouncement and ridicule, go loyally on in their work of exposing the pinks, the lavenders, and the reds who have sought refuge beneath the wings of the American Eagle."[17]

~

"Like millions of others, I honestly feared the spread of Communism to the United States and elsewhere, whether by a fifth column inside society or by armed aggression."[18]

~

In time, Graham realized that a fear of communism had prompted extreme and sometimes unjustified behavior. He moved away from some of his earlier pronouncements.

"For all of my early anti-Communist diatribes ... I certainly did not see myself as a crusader against Communism like Senator McCarthy or Father Charles Coughlin, the vocal Catholic priest who had a national radio program during the 1930s and was often criticized for his extreme right-wing political views."[19]

~

Although Graham became wary of political involvement, he once said that congressmen and even a former member of Roosevelt's cabinet had approached him to run for the United States Senate from North Carolina or perhaps the presidency in 1956. Graham declined saying that only under special circumstances would he consider running for office:

> *"If the country ever comes close to Communism, I will offer myself in any capacity to lead the Christian people of this country in the preservation of their God-given democratic institutions."*[20]

WAR

In 1966, during the Vietnam War, Billy Graham told audiences that Christians could support war: "Jesus said 'Think not that I am come to send peace on earth: I came not to send peace, but a sword.'"[21]

~

In 1967 Graham wrote to *The Christian Century* magazine protesting an article accusing him of taking an inappropriate position on the Vietnam war:

> *"I have been extremely careful not to be drawn into either the moral implications or the tactical military problems of the Vietnam War."*

The magazine continued to insist that Graham had passed judgment on the presence of U.S. military power in Vietnam, claiming that Graham "condemned

Martin Luther King, Jr.'s simultaneous involvement in the civil rights movement and in antiwar protests. He said, 'Surely Negroes are as divided about the war as the rest of us, and it [King's action] is an affront to the thousands of loyal Negro troops who are in Vietnam.'"

The magazine also accused Graham of saying that antiwar protests "so exaggerate our divisions over the war that they could make Hanoi confident that it will eventually win. Then, what already is anticipated as a long war will be even longer." Indeed, wrote the editors, "he was more specific. He said that the protesters against the war in Vietnam are 'giving comfort to the enemy.' Graham has the right to hold and express opinions on Vietnam. We wish, however, that he would do so without duplicity. He should drop either the image of holy transcendence or the mantle of concerned involvement. God alone is capable of wearing both."[22]

～

Graham, like every American, had opinions about the war:

"We tend to blame America too much and the Vietcong too little."[23]

～

Graham was asked by *Newsweek* magazine in 1973 how he felt about President Nixon's resumption of bombing North Vietnam. He responded that the world has a lot of violence that doesn't make headlines, there are many being killed by drunken drivers and crime. "But what of the bombing?" persisted *Newsweek*. Graham said he deplored the suffering and killing in the war and prayed that it could be ended as soon as possible:

> *"But we also have to realize that there are hundreds of thousands of deaths attributed to smoking. . ."*[24]

THE PRESIDENTS

Billy Graham sees the president of the United States, whomever is serving in the office, as a symbol of unity for the nation. It is Graham's hope to give spiritual support and friendship to presidents, and to steer clear of political advice or involvement:

> *"It has been my privilege to know ten presidents, some as close friends. I knew most of them before they ever became president, and have been in their homes and glimpsed their family lives. I have had long talks with them. All faced temptations and pressures most of us can hardly imagine. Don't get me wrong; most of the presidents I have known were dedicated and thoughtful men who sincerely sought to serve their country. When I learned of moral failures or compromises in some instances, it grieved me deeply."*[25]

PRESIDENT HARRY S. TRUMAN

President Truman, while in office, was one of the few presidents with whom Graham did not have a friendly relationship. After a long sought after meeting with

Truman, Graham revealed to the press the details of their talk. Truman was said to be livid about the breach of confidence and would not allow Graham into the White House again.

Truman once said: "Graham has gone off the beam. He's . . . well, I hadn't ought to say this, but he's one of those counterfeits I was telling you about. He claims he's a friend of all the presidents, but he was never a friend of mine when I was president. I just don't go for people like that. All he's interested in is getting his name in the paper."[26]

Graham, in turn, poked fun at Truman, especially for his handling of the Korean War:

"Harry is doing the best he can. The trouble is that he just can't do any better."[27]

Graham has said, however, that after Truman left the White House, the two men met at the president's home in Independence, Missouri, and got along well.

PRESIDENT DWIGHT D. EISENHOWER

Disillusioned with Truman, Graham was concerned about who the next president would be. He wrote a letter to his friend, Texas oil magnate Sid Richardson, giving a positive evaluation of General Eisenhower, expressing hope that Eisenhower would run for the presidency.

Richardson suggested that Graham write to Ike listing the reasons why he should enter the race. At first

Graham refused, saying that he couldn't get involved in politics. But on Richardson's insistence, Graham wrote the letter.

Upon reading it, Ike asked Richardson: "Who was that young preacher you had write me? It was the darndest letter I ever got. I'd like to meet him someday."

Graham requested an interview and later was credited in some circles for persuading Ike to run, although Billy says he was only one voice among many.[28]

～

Graham says he saw Eisenhower more than any other president and knew him the best. He visited Eisenhower just before his death. Ike asked him to explain how he could know his sins were forgiven and that he was going to heaven. Billy talked to him about salvation and Ike replied, "Thank you, I'm ready."[29]

NOTE: For more on Eisenhower, see the section "Racial Discrimination."

PRESIDENT JOHN F. KENNEDY

In April 1960, Graham was approached by Pierre Salinger, aide to then Senator Jack Kennedy. Salinger told Graham that Kennedy wanted a statement from him on the Roman Catholic issue to help Kennedy in the West Virginia presidential primary. Kennedy wanted Graham to say that the religious issue should play no part in the campaign and that he, Graham, would not hesitate to vote for a Catholic if he was qualified:

"I said no. I was afraid some might interpret any-thing I said on the subject as an implied political endorsement."[30]

Graham says that he later was tricked into accompanying Kennedy to a press conference at the Washington Hotel, then was surprised when Kennedy introduced him. Although Graham knew he was being used, he decided to express his opinion that there was no reason a Catholic shouldn't be elected president of the United States.

~

The last time Graham was with JFK was at the 1963 National Prayer Breakfast, just months before Kennedy was assassinated in Dallas. Graham had the flu and told Kennedy that he would keep his distance so the president wouldn't get sick.

JFK said, "Oh, I don't mind, I talk to a lot of people all day long who have got all kinds of bugs."

Afterward, they walked out from the hotel to the president's car. "At the curb he turned to me. 'Billy, could you ride back to the White House with me? I'd like to see you for a minute.'"

Graham demurred, explaining that he had a fever and felt quite ill. He suggested that they meet at a later time. It was a decision that would haunt Graham for years. What did Kennedy want to talk about?

"Should I have gone with him? It was an irrecover-able moment."[31]

~

During the second week in November 1963, just before the assassination, Graham had a premonition:

"I unaccountably felt such a burden about the presidential visit to Dallas that I decided to phone our mutual friend, Senator Smathers, to tell him I really wanted to talk to the president." A secretary told Graham that Smathers was on the Senate floor and would call Graham back. Instead, Smathers sent Graham a telegram saying that Kennedy would contact Graham directly. Smathers thought Graham wanted to reschedule a golf game that had been canceled. Graham's real message was never delivered.

"But all I wanted to tell him and the president was one thing, 'Don't go to Texas!'"[32]

~

"Kennedy was no intellectual—I mean, he was written up by the eastern press as an intellectual because he agreed with the eastern establishment. But Nixon is a true intellectual and he is a student, particularly a student of history."[33]

PRESIDENT LYNDON B. JOHNSON

"I love to be around him, because I love Texas, and he's all Texas. And I think you have to be in that Pedernales River valley to understand President Johnson. I understand a little bit of the background of where he came from and where his roots were and

what made him tick. And the things people thought
of as crude were not crude to me, because I had been
there, and I knew that that is the part of Texas he
came from."34

~

When Graham visited the Johnson ranch in 1971, the
two men walked to the family cemetery beside the
Pedernales River. "Billy," said Johnson, "one day
you're going to preach at my funeral. You'll stand
right here under this tree. I'll be buried right there.
You'll read the Bible, of course, and preach the gospel.
I want you to. But I hope you'll also tell folks some of
the things I tried to do."35

"Don't use any notes, the wind will blow them
away. And I don't want a lot of fancy eulogizing, but
be sure to mention my name."36

Then Johnson asked, "Billy, will I ever see my
mother and father again?"

"Well, Mr. President, if you're a Christian and they
were Christians, then someday you'll have a great
home-going."37

~

Two years later Graham spoke at Lyndon Johnson's
funeral, describing the former president as history in
motion:

"Johnson [was] a mountain of a man with a whirl-
wind for a heart . . . [whose] 38 years of public service
kept him at the center of events that have shaped our
destiny."38

PRESIDENT RICHARD MILHOUSE NIXON

Graham often said that although he is a Democrat and Nixon was a Republican, he thought Nixon was the best-qualified president the United States ever had.

"He and I had been personal friends for over 20 years."[39]

~

Although Graham had a policy against endorsing candidates:

"In May [1960], I spoke at the Southern Baptist Convention and made thinly veiled allusions to my preference, without giving Nixon my outright endorsement."[40]

~

But, Graham said later, that was a mistake:

"I went too far. I went too far when I did things to help him politically. I should have limited myself to the moral and spiritual situation in the country."[41]

~

When Nixon's White House tapes were released during the Watergate investigation, Graham was devastated. The tapes revealed a side of Nixon that Graham had never seen.

"I just couldn't understand it. I still can't. I thought he was a man of great integrity, I looked upon him as a possibility of leading this country to its greatest and best days. And all those people around him, they

all seemed to me so clean, family men, so clean-living. Sometimes, when I look back on it all now, it has the aspects of a nightmare."[42]

~

Graham seemed to seek justification for Nixon's crude language on the White House tapes:

"The President never dreamed that he was being recorded."[43]

~

But justifications didn't soothe the pain for Graham. For days after he listened to the Nixon tapes, Graham's mother remembers that Billy was very subdued. "There just wasn't that usual glow in Billy's face. It was like the light had gone out."[44]

~

Graham speculated that Nixon's judgment and behavior may have been distorted due to the president's dependence on sleeping pills.

"I was terribly disappointed in those tapes. Just overwhelmingly sickened by them. Oh, the language."[45]

~

After reports of Jack Kennedy's sexual antics as president, Graham said: "He [Nixon] didn't have nude women running around in the private quarters of the White House."[46]

~

"I feel sorry for the president and his family. . . . I shall always consider him a personal friend. His personal suffering must be unbearable."[47]

~

After the Watergate scandal, President Nixon returned home to San Clemente, California, and was seriously ill.

"He came close to death. My wife Ruth hired a one-motor plane to pull a sign back and forth in front of the hospital, saying GOD LOVES YOU AND SO DO WE. And nobody knew it was Ruth."[48]

PRESIDENT GERALD R. FORD

Not long after Nixon resigned and Gerald Ford became president, Graham called to tell Ford that it would initiate a healing process if he pardoned Richard Nixon. Ford replied, "Well, it's a tough call, a tough decision, there are many angles to it. I'm certainly giving it a lot of thought and prayer."

Graham said, "Mr. President, I'm praying for you constantly."

Within a few days Ford announced a pardon for Nixon.[49]

~

During Ford's tenure in the White House, Graham was seated beside the former actress Grace Kelly, then Princess Grace of Monaco:

"We were chatting, but at the same time I was stalling. I was looking in despair at the elaborate place setting of knives, forks, and spoons. She would surely know the correct one with which to start. 'Dr. Graham, are you watching me?' she asked. 'Yes,' I said, caught in the act. 'But I'm watching you,' she said, 'I'm waiting for you to start!'"[50]

PRESIDENT JIMMY CARTER

Although Graham described Carter as one of the hardest-working presidents we've ever had, the relationship did not seem warm in the beginning.

Graham once said of Carter: "I would rather have a man in office who is highly qualified to be president who didn't make much of a religious profession than to have a man who had no qualifications but who made a religious profession." Carter snapped back: "I think what people should look out for is people like Billy Graham, who go around telling people how to live their lives." After Carter won the election, Graham conceded that he "is a leader we can trust and follow."[51]

~

Graham was not at Carter's inauguration, the first he had missed since 1949, but attended a presidential Prayer Breakfast a few days later:

"Rosalyn asked if we wanted to sleep in the Lincoln Room, and I told her, 'No I don't. That bed has a hump right in the middle.' I'd been there with both

*the Johnsons and the Nixons, so I knew how the beds
slept. She said, 'Really?' She went back and felt it and
said, 'You're right.' So we slept in the Queen's Room
across the hall. The same thing happened with the
Reagans, but I think Mrs. Reagan got a new mat-
tress for the Lincoln Room."[52]*

In recent years the relationship between Graham and
Carter has been cordial. The two appeared on a Larry
King CNN talk show on the challenges of growing
older, and Graham praised Carter's recent book, *The
Virtues of Aging.*

PRESIDENT RONALD REAGAN

As he has done with other candidates, Graham refused
a request to endorse Ronald Reagan for the presidency.
Graham had known Reagan for nearly 40 years,
though, and enjoyed his natural, cheerful optimism.

~

The Grahams were staying at the Madison Hotel in
Washington and had just gone to bed when the phone
rang. It was Nancy Reagan. "Are you all asleep?" she
asked. "Just about," Graham answered. "We're in bed
too, but we want to see you both and talk to you. Can
you come over here?" "We'll have a car in front of the
hotel in 15 minutes." The Grahams spent several hours
at 1600 Pennsylvania Avenue talking with the pajama-
clad Reagans.[53]

~

When President Reagan was shot by John Hinkley, Jesse Helms called Graham and suggested that he go to Washington immediately. After praying with the president, Graham called Hinckley's parents, whom he understood were Christians, and assured them of his prayers for them "because I knew their hearts must have been breaking."[54]

PRESIDENT GEORGE W. BUSH

Graham says Bush was the easiest president of all with which to discuss spiritual matters, since he openly proclaims his Christianity.

On January 16, 1991, Graham received an urgent phone call asking him to come to the White House immediately for lunch with President Bush. Graham said there wasn't time to get there from North Carolina. Soon afterward another call came requesting his presence for dinner. Graham rushed to Washington:

"I had just showered and changed clothes when Barbara Bush tapped on my door with her cane. 'Welcome!' she said. 'How about pushing me down to the Blue Room, and we'll watch television together?'" (Wheelchair bound, the first lady was recovering from a fall off a sled while playing with her grandchildren.)

"In the Blue Room, which was made cozy with family pictures and personal mementos, we watched CNN . . . All of a sudden, the commentators in Baghdad, Peter Arnett and Bernard Shaw, exclaimed that

anti-aircraft fire was going up. . . . I turned to Barbara. 'Is this the beginning of the war?' I asked. She did not say anything. About 15 minutes later the President came into the room and sat down to watch television. He confirmed the war had started."[55]

PRESIDENT WILLIAM JEFFERSON CLINTON
Graham says he has known Bill Clinton for many years:

"I think a lot of him. But I am very disappointed in him."[56]

～

After the president acknowledged an inappropriate relationship with Monica Lewinsky, Billy Graham had a meeting with him:

"I try to be a pastor, those conversations are private."

～

Graham declared that he still loves Clinton as a friend:

"I pray for him every day, I pray for Hillary every day, and I pray for Chelsea especially."[57]

～

In defending Bill Clinton, Graham asks us to remember that Clinton is "a strong, vigorous young man with such a tremendous personality that ladies just go wild over him. He's had a lot of temptations thrown his way and a lot of pressure on him. Oh, it must be tough—and," Graham added, "I know how hard it is."[58]

～

During an NBC interview, Graham said that the accusations of adultery against Clinton should be put into perspective: "You must bear in mind that there are ten commandments. This is one of the ten."

The Canadian magazine *MacLeans* asked, "Just one of ten. What's everyone so excited about?"[59]

～

MacLeans has long been suspicious of Graham's fondness for presidents: "A highlight film of Billy's life would be him on the golf course with a president. Miraculously, if we may use the term, he managed to befriend Republican and Democrat presidents alike and always showed up on the golf course with them. This may indicate a vast tolerance. Others might think it a photo opportunity.[60]

～

Graham lead a crusade in Little Rock, Arkansas, during the racial unrest of the early 1960s, and insisted on preaching to an intergrated audience. A 12-year-old Bill Clinton was in the audience. The next time Graham came to Little Rock, Clinton was governor of the state.

"I'll never forget that when Billy Graham came back to Little Rock 30 years later," said Clinton, "probably the most well-known man of God and faith in the world, he took time out one day to let me take him to see my pastor [W. O. Vaught] who he'd known 30 years before, because he was dying. And my elderly pastor, with only a few weeks to live, sat and talked to Billy Graham about their life, their work, their trips to the Holy Land, and life to come. There was no one there. There were no cameras, there were no reporters, there was nothing to be gained. It was a simple, private, personal expression of common Christianity and gratitude for the life of a person who had given his life for their shared faith."[61]

OTHER WORLD LEADERS

From the time of his first crusade outside the United States in 1954, Billy Graham has been welcomed in other countries by political leaders and royalty, ranging from Queen Elizabeth II to Chinese premier Lei Pong.

In 1954, while in England on a crusade, Graham was invited at short notice to 10 Downing Street to meet Prime Minister Winston Churchill. Churchill congratulated Graham for drawing such large crowds to Wembley Stadium.

"Oh, well, it's God's doing, believe me."

"That may be," said Churchill, "but I daresay if I brought Marilyn Monroe over here, and she and I together went to Wembley, we couldn't fill it."[62]

~

Churchill asked Graham: "What hope do you have for the world?"

Graham took out his New Testamant and answered: "Mr. Prime Minister, I am filled with hope."

Churchill pointed to a stack of newspapers that were

filled with horrible stories of violence and political turmoil. "I am an old man, without hope for the world."

"Life is very exciting even if there's a war, because I know what is going to happen in the future," said Graham.

Churchill and Graham talked for 30 to 40 minutes, well beyond the allotted 5 minutes for the visit. At last Churchill stood up and again expressed his pessimism. The only hope, said the legendary war leader and prime minister: "We must have a return to God."[63]

Churchill asked Graham if their conversation had been confidential, and Billy, remembering his experience with President Truman, assured the prime minister that it was.

～

Graham visited with United Nations President Dag Hammarskjold, who soon afterward died in a plane crash. Hammarskjold was as discouraged about world peace as Churchill was. "Unless the world has a spiritual rebirth within the next few years, civilization is doomed," Hammarskjold said.[64]

～

Graham and Grady Wilson were playing golf on a course near Versailles, France, during the 1955 crusade, when someone called his name. "Dr. Graham, I heard you on television last night, and my wife and I were very interested. I'm playing golf, and we have only two in our party. Would you and your friend like to join us?" It was the Duke of Windsor.

Unfortunately, Graham could not cancel a prior commitment, so he was unable to play golf with one of the most famous romantic couples in the world.[65]

~

In 1994, when the United States and North Korea were at odds over Korea's nuclear weapons-building capabilities, Graham traveled to North Korea on a private, goodwill visit. Graham carried a message to North Korean leader Kim Il Sung from President Clinton. The message held out the possibility of better relations once the nuclear issue was resolved. Upon receiving the message, Kim Il Sung replied that Clinton had the logic reversed. The two presidents should establish a relationship first, then talk about problems. The message, according to a Korean expert who accompanied Graham, "was too short, too cool, and too blunt to be polite from a Korean point of view."

Even so, Graham and Kim Il Sung talked earnestly for another half hour, with the North Korean shaking his fist for emphasis and shouting. Graham talked about the pressure that forced Bill Clinton to be less flexible: "He's doing the best he can, under the circumstances."

He chatted with Kim Il Sung as one old man to another about young men who can sometimes be brash. Graham appeared to convince Kim Il Sung that Clinton was sincere.

A few weeks later, Kim Il Sung agreed to allow international inspectors access to the nuclear sites.[66]

~

During a visit to the British royal family, Graham explained:

"I preached in utter simplicity. . . . I had prayed so much that I knew that however simple and full of mistakes my sermon was, God would overrule it and use it."[67]

~

Graham once asked a Chinese Communist leader: "Why is Christianity growing so fast in China?"

He responded, "Persecution. If you want to evangelize China, just persecute Christians. The more they are persecuted, the faster the church grows."[68]

~

In addition to political leaders, throughout his career Graham has enjoyed the support of many opinion leaders, entertainers, and authors. Johnny Cash and the Carter Family singers frequently entertained at Graham sermons, as did the Christian singers Ethel Waters and Andrea Crouch. Phyllis George, Roy Rogers and his wife, Dale Evans, and the author Corrie ten Boom also appeared on the stage with Graham.

Comedian Bob Hope said of Graham: "Billy is the most honorable man I have ever met. He's a dear friend and we love it when he plays golf in the Desert Classic [in Palm Springs, California] . . . we use him for earthquake insurance."[69]

~

THE CRITICS

As beloved as he is by many people, Billy Graham also has many critics.

> *"I am hated in some areas. Why I even have to watch what I say on the telephone now. I even watch what I say to my wife at home. They've got this electronic equipment now, microphones that they could aim at you from some mountaintop around here five miles away—and they could pick up absolutely everything you're saying in your own bedroom. I even watch what I say to my wife in our own bedroom now."[1]*

THE FUNDAMENTALISTS

Fundamentalist religious leader Bob Jones expressed the feelings of some fundamentalists when he said that "Graham has done more harm to the cause of Christ than any other living man."[2]

～

"The grand irony in his career," wrote Martin E. Marty of the Toronto *Star Tribune*, "and one that grieves Graham—is that the most enduring resistance by the unmelted comes from people on his right, fundamentalists of the hard line with whom he associated at the beginning. They see him as a sellout who compromises his Christ by keeping company with agnostics, Jews, Catholics, moderate Protestants, the worldly and not-yet or never-won converts."[3]

～

Billy Graham acknowledges the problem:

"Fundamentalist is a grand and wonderful word, but it got off track and into so many extreme positions. . . . I felt like my own brother had turned against me."[4]

～

"We think of a fundamentalist [as someone] who says, 'I believe in Christ,' and he says it with a snarl. But there are many that are wonderful people."[5]

～

Graham takes pride in the fact that he opens his crusades to all denominations and refers his converts back to the church doctrine of their own choosing:

"In all my years of evangelism I have never urged people to join a particular denomination. The important thing is for everyone to join a church where they

can grow spiritually, and every man must determine this for himself."[6]

～

At a meeting of evangelists, Graham called some of his fundamentalist critics "extremists" and said to them: "I would like to make myself clear. I intend to go anywhere, sponsored by anybody, to preach the gospel of Christ, if there are no strings attached to my message. I am sponsored by civic clubs, universities, ministerial associations, and councils of churches all over the world. I intend to continue. The one badge of Christian discipleship is not orthodoxy, but love. . . . Christians are not limited to any church. The only question is: Are you committed to Christ?"[7]

～

The conservative organization, Bible Discernment Ministries, often is critical of Graham. The group was disturbed by his comments on a July 1993 interview on ABC-TV's *Good Morning America*:

"I'm delighted the Pope is coming [to Denver]. . . . I admire the Pope though I don't agree with him on everything. . . ."

Then the Ministries added: "The Pope in talks this year insists that he is the infallible 'Vicar of Christ.' How can anyone who proclaims the one and only true gospel ever be 'delighted' that a counterfeit Christ would come with a false gospel to beguile thousands of youth?"[8]

~

While Graham welcomes interaction with all different styles of Christianity, he is clear in his own mind that to be a Christian, an individual must accept Jesus Christ as his savior. On this point he has no tolerance at all. In fact, there are many situations, says Graham, where too much broad-mindedness is a bad thing:

> *"Once, while on a plane traveling to Japan, we flew through a rough snowstorm. When we arrived over the airport in Tokyo, the visibility was almost zero. The pilot had to make an instrument landing. I did not want that pilot to be broad-minded. I wanted him to be narrow-minded. I knew that our lives depended on it."[9]*

~

The way to salvation is as certain as science, and science is specific:

> *"There is no room for careless broad-mindedness in the laboratory. Water boils at 212 degrees Fahrenheit at sea level; it is never 100 degrees or at 189 degrees, but always at 212. Water freezes at 32 degrees Fahrenheit at sea level; it is never at 23 or 31 degrees."[10]*

THE LIBERALS

Graham is sometimes attacked by mainstream Christians. In 1950 in Portland, Oregon, a group of "liberal" ministers expressed puzzlement over Graham's success. The magazine *The Christian Century* ran an account: "They agreed that Graham is sincere, but deplored his theological literalism and his personality, his sensationalism, his publicity techniques and his burning conviction that he is indeed a latter-day prophet."[11]

∿

During the social awakening of the late 1950s, some religious writers saw Graham's philosophy as one that could create a chasm between members of the community.

Reinhold Niebuhr criticized Graham for the lack of love and justice in Graham's racial message, and the shortcomings of evangelistic preaching regarding social issues: ". . . the question arises why an obviously honest man, such as Graham, cannot embody the disavowal of race prejudice into his call to repentance. Perhaps the answer to that question takes one into the very heart of the weaknesses of 'evangelical' Christianity, particularly of evangelical Christianity in its pietistic versions. This form of Christian faith relies on an oversimplification of the issues in order to create the 'crisis' which prompts conversion and the acceptance of the Christian faith," Niebuhr wrote in *The Christian Century* magazine.[12]

∿

Niebuhr quoted a Jewish friend who witnessed one of Graham's revivals in Richmond, Virginia: "We Jews are naturally critical not only because such a revival, with its emphasis upon a commitment in religious terms to which Jews cannot subscribe, tends to widen the chasm between Jews and Christians, which common devotion to civic decencies has tended to bridge, but also because the commitment does not include a new attitude on the race issue, which is so desperately needed today."[13]

~

"The personal achievements of Graham as a Christian and as an evangelist should be fully appreciated," Niebuhr wrote in another article. "But they do not materially alter the fact that an individualistic approach to faith and commitment, inevitable as it may be, is in danger both of obscuring the highly complex tasks of justice in the community and of making too sharp distinction between the 'saved' and the 'unsaved.' The latter may not have signed a decision card but may have accepted racial equality with greater grace than the saved."[14]

Although Graham never altered his basic belief about Christian conversion, he strove to promote peace and tolerance.

~

Graham's frequent attempts to steer clear of politics led to the charge that he is unconcerned about social issues:

"My belief in the social implications of the gospel has deepened and broadened. . . . I am convinced that faith without works is dead."

Graham added that he "never felt that the accusations against me of having no social concern were valid."[15]

～

One British critic said of Graham: "His theology is 50 years behind contemporary scholarship. He gives no sign of having read any of it from the last three decades. He is completely out of step with the majority of ministers and pastors."[16]

～

Despite detractors Graham has strong support in most religious communities.

". . . evangelical theologians applaud Graham for his unhesitating proclamation of a fully reliable Scripture, his focus on the Christological center of the Bible, his demonstration of the converting power of the gospel, his fervent vision of the duty of global evangelism, and his insistence that the fallen human race faces an awesome dual destiny in eternity that only belief in Christ can infuse with hope," wrote Carl C. F. Henry in *Christianity Today*. "For a non-theologian, that is a hefty contribution, and we must all be grateful to God for it."[17]

～

Graham's critics aren't limited to conservative and liberal Christians, however. In 1960, African witch doctors picketed preliminary meetings for the Billy

Graham crusade in Kisumu, a town 165 miles north of Nairobi, Kenya. A member of Graham's advance team warned him that "for the past three days native medicine men have been parading outside the meeting in their weird costumes, muttering incantations."[18] Graham traveled on to Kisumu anyway and his service went forward without incident.

∼

LOOKING BACK ON
A LONG LIFE

A college student once asked Billy Graham what his greatest surprise in life had been:

"The brevity of life. I never realized that life would pass so quick, and go so fast."[1]

~

Asked about significant changes in the American church scene in the last 25 years, Graham said the most notable change was the emergence of evangelicalism as a significant worldwide movement. The second was the birth of many new parachurch organizations, or independent Christian groups, working alongside traditional faiths.

"Third is the new understanding between Roman Catholics and Protestants. Twenty-five years ago we could hardly speak with each other openly. In our crusades today, thousands of Catholics feel free to attend. I have preached in Roman Catholic

schools, and have even received honorary doctorates from them. This could not have happened 25 years ago."²

~

"I've lost some of the rigidity I once had, there are still some people who think that Christians must be in revolt against any government that is not Christian. But that's not what we find in the Bible. The prophet Daniel served in a pagan court, and the Jews and Christians both adjusted to the administration of the Roman Empire."³

~

"I used to play God, but I can't do that anymore. I used to believe that pagans in far-off countries were lost—were going to hell—if they did not have the gospel of Jesus Christ preached to them. I no longer believe that. I believe that there are other ways of recognizing the existence of God—through nature, for instance—and plenty of other opportunities, therefore, of saying 'yes' to God."⁴

~

"How I wish I could take back some of the statements made in those early days because of immaturity or a lack of knowledge or experience. Many of those early statements were lifted out of context by some critics and used to ridicule the message as a whole. Then there were some misquotations which I still have to face and live down. For example, one evening in Pasadena I quoted the then Secretary of

the Air Force to the effect that America had two years in which to prepare. The next day a wire service sent across the country a report saying that I had predicted the end of the world in two years."[5]

~

"This is where I think I failed in my earlier ministry—I didn't emphasize enough what it costs to follow Christ. That's something I've learned from traveling to other countries and from my American critics."[6]

~

"I have listened to too many sermons, read too many Christian books, and seen too many Christian films with happily-ever-after endings. Some even declare that if you become a Christian you will get rich or always be successful. In our attempts to share the faith we have given the impression that once you have accepted Christ as Savior and Lord, your problems are over. This is not true. Becoming 'new' in Christ is a wonderful beginning, but it isn't the end of pain or problems in our lives. It is the beginning of our facing up to them. Being a Christian involves a life time of hard work, dedicated study, and difficult decisions."[7]

~

"In my younger days, I really *thought the world could be saved. I experienced many discouragements before I realized that this was a theological mistake. Christ never taught that we would see the conversion*

of the world. . . . Noah preached for 120 years and did not have a single convert."[8]

~

"Endurance, perseverance, and dedication in fulfilling the task of an evangelist result in the most wonderful of all rewards. Nothing in this world can be more thrilling than to hear the Lord saying 'Well done, thou good and faithful servant'."[9]

~

Graham, then age 79, appeared on the Larry King television talk show. King asked him if people now treated him like an older person.

"I have Parkinson's disease. And that makes me stumble and sometimes I can keep myself from trembling a little bit or showing a weakness, especially when I am walking or stepping up to a stage. So when I get up to preach, I'm glad to have a pulpit to hold on to. And people can't tell that I'm getting old yet. But they will pretty soon."

Does that bother him? King asked.

"No. It doesn't bother me because this is where I am sure the Lord wants me to be. Maybe I can set an example to other people that are going through this sort of thing. The Pope has Parkinson's and Miss [Attorney General Janet] Reno has Parkinson's and Muhammad Ali has Parkinson's. And they have all three been an example to me as how to keep going and how to keep your smile, even in the midst of suf-

fering with this disease, because there's no cure to this disease."[10]

~

"I'm not going to retire unless my board of directors tells me, 'You're getting senile . . .' I was called by the Lord, and he didn't give any specifications on age. The Apostle John preached into his nineties. Most of the apostles preached until they were killed or died. And that's the way I intend to do it."[11]

~

"Oh, certainly I have given [retirement] thought. My wife and I have discussed it. And I have discussed it with some of my children, but I am going to continue to go on. And they agree, until the Lord removes me."[12]

Graham collapsed in Toronto in 1995 and was hospitalized. It was announced later that year that his eldest son, Franklin, would take charge when Billy is gone. Franklin now heads the worldwide Christian mission organization, Samaritan's Purse, and preaches at crusades in small U.S. cities. It took Franklin a while to decide to take up his father's work. At a 1990 crusade in Little Rock, Arkansas, Franklin talked about his own work:

"All of my father's adult life he has committed his ministry to crusade evangelism, coming to cities such as this to proclaim the gospel of Jesus Christ. Well, up to this point God hasn't called me to the large cities

175

and stadiums such as this, but he's called me to the gutters of the world. To the famine areas, to the war areas. We go to places like Beirut. We go to places like Angola and Mozambique and Ethiopia, looking for ways to help people who are suffering."[13]

∼

Regardless of the future of his religious organization, Billy Graham describes a clear idea of his own future:

"Finally, the way of salvation has not changed. I know how the ending of the book will be. The gospel that built this school and the gospel that brings me here tonight is still the way to salvation."[14]

∼

Graham looks forward to that moment when God's plan is revealed on a "big screen in the sky, a panorama of history."[15]

"Someday we will know everything."[16]

∼

Billy and Ruth Graham have chosen a secluded spot on the property of The Cove Training Center where they will be buried someday.

"I'm looking forward to death, I'll be very happy to get out of this body and into the new world that's being prepared. It'll be a feeling of tremendous joy and relief and rest. The Bible says I have not seen nor heard, nor has there entered the mind of man, what God has in store for us in the future life."[17]

~

Asked by David Frost whom he would like to preach at his funeral:

> *"I might preach it myself and put it on tape and let people see me preach at my own funeral. Then I'd tell some things that they never knew before."*[18]

LIST OF CRUSADES, 1947 TO 1999

1947 Grand Rapids, Michigan
Charlotte, North Carolina

1948 Augusta, Georgia
Modesto, California

1949 Miami, Florida
Baltimore, Maryland
Altoona, Pennsylvania
Los Angeles, California

1950 Boston, Massachusetts
Columbia, South Carolina
New England States Tour
Portland, Oregon
Minneapolis, Minnesota
Atlanta, Georgia

1951 Southern States Tour:
Fort Worth, Texas

Shreveport, Louisiana
Memphis, Tennessee

Seattle, Washington
Hollywood, California
Greensboro, North Carolina
Raleigh, North Carolina

1952 Washington, D.C.
Houston, Texas
Jackson, Mississippi
Pittsburgh, Pennsylvania
Albuquerque, New Mexico

1953 Chattanooga, Tennessee
St. Louis, Missouri
Dallas, Texas
Syracuse, New York
Detroit, Michigan
Asheville, North Carolina

1954 London, England
Amsterdam, The Netherlands
Berlin, West Germany
Copenhagen, Denmark
Dusseldorf, West Germany
Frankfurt, West Germany
Helsinki, Finland
Paris, France

Stockholm, Sweden

Nashville, Tennessee

New Orleans, Louisiana

1955 Glasgow, Scotland

London, England

Paris, France

Zurich, Switzerland

Geneva, Switzerland

Mannheim, West Germany

Stuttgart, West Germany

Nurnberg, West Germany

Dortmund, West Germany

Frankfurt, West Germany

U.S. Service Bases

Rotterdam, The Netherlands

Oslo, Norway

Gothenburg, Sweden

Aarhus, Denmark

Toronto, Ontario, Canada

1956 India and the Far East Tour

Richmond, Virginia

Oklahoma City, Oklahoma

Louisville, Kentucky

1957 New York City, New York

1958 Caribbean Tour

San Francisco, California

Sacramento, California

Fresno, California

Santa Barbara, California

Los Angeles, California

San Diego, California

San Antonio, Texas

Charlotte, North Carolina

1959 Melbourne, Australia

Auckland, New Zealand

Sydney, Australia

Perth, Australia

Brisbane, Australia

Adelaide, Australia

Wellington, New Zealand

Christchurch, New Zealand

Canberra, Launceton, Hobart, Australia

Little Rock, Arkansas

Wheaton, Illinois

Indianapolis, Indiana

1960 Monrovia, Liberia

Accra, Ghana

Kumasi, Ghana

Lagos, Nigeria

Ibadan, Nigeria

Kaduna, Nigeria

Enugu, Nigeria

Jos, Nigeria

Bulawayo, South Rhodesia

Salisbury, Rhodesia

Kitwe, North Rhodesia

Moshi, Tanganyika

Kisumu, Kenya

Usumbura, Ruanda-Urundi

Nairobi, Kenya

Addis Ababa, Ethiopia

Cairo, Egypt

Middle-East Tour

Washington, D.C.

Rio de Janeiro, Brazil

Bern, Switzerland

Zurich, Switzerland

Basel, Switzerland

Lausanne, Switzerland

Essen, West Germany

Hamburg, West Germany

Berlin, West Germany

New York City (Spanish)

1961 Jacksonville, Florida

Orlando, Florida

Clearwater, Florida

St. Petersburg, Florida

Tampa, Florida

Bradenton-Sarasota, Florida

Tallahassee, Florida

Gainesville, Florida

Miami, Florida

Cape Canaveral, Florida

West Palm Beach, Florida

Vero Beach, Florida

Peace River Park, Florida

Boca Raton, Florida

Fort Lauderdale, Florida

Manchester, England

Glasgow, Scotland

Belfast, Northern Ireland

Minneapolis, Minnesota

Philadelphia, Pennsylvania

1962 South America Tour

Chicago, Illinois

Fresno, California

Redstone Arsenal, Alabama

El Paso, Texas

1963 Paris, France

Lyon, France

Toulouse, France

Mulhouse, France

Nurnberg, West Germany

Stuttgart, West Germany

Los Angeles, California

1964 Birmingham, Alabama

Phoenix, Arizona

San Diego, California

Columbus, Ohio

Omaha, Nebraska

Boston, Massachusetts

Manchester, New Hampshire

Portland, Maine

Bangor, Maine

Providence, Rhode Island

Louisville, Kentucky

1965 Honolulu, Oahu

Kahului, Maui

Hilo, Hawaii

Lihue, Kauai

Dothan, Alabama

Tuscaloosa, Alabama

University of Alabama

Auburn, Alabama

Auburn University

Tuskegee Institute, Alabama

Montgomery, Alabama

Copenhagen, Denmark

Vancouver, British Columbia, Canada

Seattle, Washington

Denver, Colorado

Houston, Texas

1966 Greenville, South Carolina
London, England
Berlin, West Germany

1967 Ponce, Puerto Rico
San Juan, Puerto Rico
Winnipeg, Manitoba, Canada
Great Britain
Turin, Italy
Zagreb, Yugoslavia
Toronto, Ontario, Canada
Kansas City, Missouri
Tokyo, Japan

1968 Brisbane, Australia
Sydney, Australia
Portland, Oregon
San Antonio, Texas
Pittsburgh, Pennsylvania

1969 Auckland, New Zealand
Dunedin, New Zealand
Melbourne, Australia
New York City, New York
Anaheim, California

1970 Dortmund, West Germany
Knoxville, Tennessee

New York City, New York
Baton Rouge, Louisiana

1971 Lexington, Kentucky
Chicago, Illinois
Oakland, California
Dallas-Ft.Worth, Texas

1972 Charlotte, North Carolina
Birmingham, Alabama
Cleveland, Ohio
Kohima, Nagaland, India

1973 Durban, South Africa
Johannesburg, South Africa
Seoul, South Korea
Atlanta, Georgia
Minneapolis-St. Paul, Minnesota
Raleigh, North Carolina
St. Louis, Missouri

1974 Phoenix, Arizona
Los Angeles, California
Rio de Janeiro, Brazil
Norfolk-Hampton, Virginia

1975 Albuquerque, New Mexico
Jackson, Mississippi
Brussels, Belgium
Lubbock, Texas

Taipei, Taiwan
Hong Kong

1976 Seattle, Washington
Williamsburg, Virginia
San Diego, California
Detroit, Michigan
Nairobi, Kenya

1977 Gothenburg, Sweden
Asheville, North Carolina
South Bend, Indiana
Hungary Tour
Cincinnati, Ohio
Manila, Phillippines
India (Good News Festivals)

1978 Las Vegas, Nevada
Memphis, Tennessee
Toronto, Ontario, Canada
Kansas City, Missouri
Oslo, Norway
Stockholm, Sweden
Poland Tour
Singapore

1979 São Paulo, Brazil
Tampa, Florida
Sydney, Australia
Nashville, Tennessee

Milwaukee, Wisconsin

Halifax, Nova Scotia, Canada

1980 Oxford, England

Cambridge, England

Indianapolis, Indiana

Edmonton, Alberta, Canada

Wheaton, Illinois

Okinawa, Japan

Osaka, Japan

Fukuoka, Japan

Tokyo, Japan

Reno, Nevada

Las Vegas, Nevada

1981 Mexico City, Mexico

Villahermosa, Mexico

Boca Raton, Florida

Baltimore, Maryland

Calgary, Alberta, Canada

San Jose, California

Houston, Texas

1982 Blackpool, England

Providence, Rhode Island

Burlington, Vermont

Portland, Maine

Springfield, Massachusetts

Manchester, New Hampshire

Hartford, Connecticut

New Haven, Connecticut

New England University and College Lecture Tour:

Northeastern University, Boston, Massachusetts

University of Massachusetts, Amherst,
    Massachusetts

Yale University, New Haven, Connecticut

Harvard University, Cambridge, Massachusetts

Boston College, Newton, Massachusetts

Massachusetts Institute of Technology,
    Cambridge, Massachusetts

Gordon-Conwell Seminary, South Hamilton,
    Massachusetts

Dartmouth College, Hanover, New Hampshire

Boston, Massachusetts

Boise, Idaho

Spokane, Washington

Chapel Hill, North Carolina

Wittenberg, German Democratic Republic

Dresden, German Democratic Republic

Gorlitz, German Democratic Republic

Stendal, German Democratic Republic

Stralsund, German Democratic Republic

Berlin, German Democratic Republic

Prague, Czechoslovakia

Brno, Czechoslovakia

Bratislava, Czechoslovakia

Nassau, Bahamas

1983 Orlando, Florida

Tacoma, Washington

Sacramento, California

Oklahoma City, Oklahoma

1984 Anchorage, Alaska

Bristol, England

Sunderland, England

Norwich, England

Birmingham, England

Liverpool, England

Ipswich, England

Seoul, South Korea

Leningrad, Russia

Tallinn, Estonia

Novosibirsk, Estonia

Moscow, Russia

Vancouver, British Columbia, Canada

1985 Fort Lauderdale, Florida

Hartford, Connecticut

Sheffield, England

Anaheim, California

Suceava, Romania

Cluj-Napoca, Romania

Oradea, Romania

Arad, Romania

Timisoara, Romania

Sibiu, Romania

Bucharest, Romania

Pecs, Hungary

Budapest, Hungary

1986 Washington, D.C.

Paris, France

Tallahassee, Florida

1987 Columbia, South Carolina

Cheyenne, Wyoming

Fargo, North Dakota

Billings, Montana

Sioux Falls, South Dakota

Denver, Colorado

Helsinki, Finland

1988 Beijing, People's Republic of China

Huaiyin, People's Republic of China

Nanjing, People's Republic of China

Shanghai, People's Republic of China

Guangzhou, People's Republic of China

Zagorsk, Russia

Moscow, Russia

Kiev, Ukraine

Buffalo, New York

Rochester, New York

Hamilton, Ontario, Canada

1989 Syracuse, New York

London, England

Budapest, Hungary
Little Rock, Arkansas

1990 Berlin, West Germany
Albany, New York
Long Island, New York
Hong Kong

1991 Seattle, Washington
Tacoma, Washington
Edinburgh, Scotland
Aberdeen, Scotland
Glasgow, Scotland
East Rutherford, New Jersey
New York, New York
Buenos Aires, Argentina

1992 Pyongyang, North Korea
Philadelphia, Pennsylvania
Portland, Oregon
Moscow, Russia

1993 Essen, Germany
Pittsburgh, Pennsylvania
Columbus, Ohio

1994 Tokyo, Japan
Beijing, People's Republic of China
Pyongyang, North Korea
Cleveland, Ohio
Atlanta, Georgia

1995 San Juan, Puerto Rico
Toronto, Ontario, Canada
Sacramento, California

1996 Minneapolis-St.Paul, Minnesota
Charlotte, North Carolina

1997 San Antonio, Texas
San Jose, California
San Francisco, California
Oakland, California

1998 Ottowa, Canada
Tampa, Florida

1999 *(Planned Crusades)*
Indianapolis, Indiana
St. Louis, Missouri

TIMELINE

1918 William Franklin Graham was born in Charlotte, North Carolina, on November 7.

1934 Billy Graham made his commitment to Christ at a revival meeting in November.

1936 Billy Graham graduated from high school and became a Fuller Brush salesman.

Later in the year he enrolled in Bob Jones College in Tennessee.

1937 After leaving Bob Jones College and enrolling in Florida Bible Institute, Graham preached his first sermon at Bostwick Baptist Church in Florida.

1938 Graham held his first revival at the East Palatka Baptist Church in Florida

1939 Graham was ordained to the ministry at Peniel Baptist Church (Florida) in the Southern Baptist Convention.

1940 Billy Graham graduated from the Florida Bible Institute (now Trinity College).

Graham enrolled in Wheaton College in Wheaton, Illinois, where he met fellow student Ruth McCue Bell, the daughter of a medical missionary who was serving in China where she was born.

1943 After graduating with a bachelor of arts degree from Wheaton College, on August 13, Graham married Ruth Bell.

1943 Western Springs Baptist Church, Western Springs, Illinois, hired Graham for his first job as a pastor.

1944 Graham began a radio program, *Songs in the Night*, through a radio station WCFL in Chicago, Illinois.

At a Youth for Christ rally in Chicago, Graham preached to his first large crowd.

1945 Graham became the charter vice president of Youth for Christ International, Chicago, to minister to WWII veterans returning to college. He served as a full-time UFC evangelist until 1950.

Graham's daughter Virginia (called Gigi) was born.

1947 Under some duress from the dying school president, Graham was named head of Northwestern Schools in Minneapolis, which consisted of three institutions: a liberal arts college, Bible school, and theological seminary. He held the job until 1952 but spent little time at the school.

1948 Daughter Anne Morrow was born.

In a California hotel room, Graham and his team agreed to the "Modesto Manifesto," guidelines for handling temptations that had brought down other evangelists.

1949 Newspaperman William Randolph Hearst raised Graham's profile, telling editors to "puff Graham," after the publisher heard him preach during the Los Angeles Canvas Crusade.

1950 The Billy Graham Evangelistic Association was founded in Minneapolis, Minnesota.

Graham also began the weekly "Hour of Decision" radio program, which is still heard on more than 900 stations worldwide.

Graham started a film company, Worldwide Pictures.

Daughter Ruth Bell Graham was born.

Graham visited President Truman in the White House, his first presidential visit.

1952 William Franklin Graham, Jr. was born.

Billy Graham became the author of syndicated newspaper column "My Answer" carried by newspapers across the country with a combined circulation of 5 million readers. Graham's book *Peace with God* was published. To date it has sold more than 2 million copies.

1953 Graham resigned as president of Northwestern Schools to concentrate on crusades.

In a bold move for the time, Graham banned seating based on race at his rallies.

1954 Graham's first London crusade attracted 2 million people in 12 weeks.

1955 Graham authored the book *The Secret of Happiness*.

1956 Graham conceived of and launched the magazine *Christianity Today*.

1957 Accepting an invitation from liberal Protestants, Graham held a massive crusade in New York City.

1958 Nelson Edman, Graham's second son, was born.

1960 Graham launched *Decision* magazine.

Graham's third book, *My Answer*, was published.

1965 Graham's new book, *World Aflame*, made the *The New York Times* and *Time* magazine bestseller lists for several weeks.

1969 Graham's book *The Challenge* was published.

Graham preached his first White House church service at the request of the newly inaugurated President Nixon.

1971 Billy Graham's book *The Jesus Generation* was published.

1972 Graham met with all sides of the conflict in Northern Ireland, including the Irish Republican Army.

1973 In what was the largest public religious service in history, Graham preached to 1,120,000 people in Korea.

1975 Graham's new book, *Angels: God's Secret Agents*, was on the bestseller lists of *Publishers Weekly* and *The New York Times* for 21 weeks each. It won an award from Evangelical Christian Publishers Association, the ECPA Platinum Book Award.

1977 Graham wrote and published *How to Be Born Again*.

1978 His newest book—*The Holy Spirit*—won the ECPA Gold Book Award.

1979 Graham influenced the founding of the Evangelical Council for Financial Accountability, a group credited with opening up and cleaning up parachurch finances.

1981 Graham's book *Till Armageddon* received the ECPA Platinum Book Award.

Pope John Paul II met with Graham at the Vatican.

Billy Graham ministered to President Reagan at his bedside after the president was shot in an assassination attempt.

1982 Graham preached for the first time in Russia.

1983 *Approaching Hoofbeats: The Four Horsemen of the Apocalypse* by Billy Graham was on *The New York*

Times bestseller list and won the ECPA Gold Book Award.

Graham was awarded the Presidential Medal of Freedom, the nation's highest civilian honor, by President Reagan.

1984 Graham's book *Peace with God* was revised and expanded.

Graham also wrote a new book, *A Biblical Standard for Evangelists*.

1986 Graham wrote another book, *Unto the Hills*.

1987 Graham's newest book, *Facing Death and the Life After*, became the Christian Booksellers Association bestseller for 21 weeks.

Billy Graham Training Center at The Cove, a Bible retreat and youth camp set in the Blue Ridge Mountains of North Carolina, opened near the Grahams' home.

1988 Graham published *Answers to Life's Problems*.

Graham preached in China and visited his wife's birthplace.

1990 Graham joined *Life* magazine's list of "The 100 Most Important Americans of the Twentieth Century."

1991 *Hope for the Troubled Heart* by Billy Graham was published.

President George Bush requested that Graham come to the White House for the launch of the war against Iraq.

Billy Graham hosted nearly 5,000 pastors and church workers at his five-day School of Evangelism in Moscow.

1992 The new Graham book this year was *Storm Warning*.

1993 Billy Graham gathered 3,900 evangelists from around the world for a conference in Amsterdam.

1995 The 77-year-old evangelist collapsed in Toronto. After being hospitalized, Graham was told to lighten his schedule.

It was announced that Graham's son Franklin would take over his ministry after Billy Graham dies.

1996 Billy and Ruth Graham jointly received the Congressional Gold Medal at the Capitol Rotunda.

1997 Billy Graham's most recent book, *Just As I Am*, a memoir of his life, was published.

NOTES

Preface

1. Richard N. Ostling, "Religion: Power, Glory and Politics," *Time*, February 17, 1998, p. 62.

2. "Clintons Top Poll of Most Admired," The Associated Press, New York, December 31, 1998.

3. Sherwood Eliot Wirt, *Billy: A Personal Look at Billy Graham, the World's Best-Loved Evangelist* (Wheaton, Illinois: Crossway Books, 1997), inside cover.

4. Martin E. Marty, "Reflections on Graham by a Former Grump," *Christianity Today*, November 18, 1988, p. 24.

5. Andrew Wark, "Graham Pays Historic Visit to North Korea," *Christianity Today*, May 18, 1992, p. 54.

6. William Martin, "Fifty Years With Billy," *Christianity Today*, November 13, 1995, p. 27.

7. "Billy Graham: The Man At Home," *The Saturday Evening Post*, Spring 1972, p. 107.

8. Philip Yancey, "Christian McCarthyism," *Christianity Today*, July 18, 1994, p. 72.

Making of an Evangelist

1. Billy Graham, "Billy Graham's Own Story, God is My Witness, Part I," *McCall's*, April 1964, p. 125.

2. Margaret Shannon, "Where Billy Graham's Sawdust Trail Begins," *The Atlanta Journal and Constitution Magazine*, January 25, 1970, p. 8.

3. Biography.com, November 25, 1998, p. 1.

4. "Billy Graham: The Man at Home," *Saturday Evening Post*, Spring 1972, p. 47.

5. Billy Graham, "Billy Graham's Own Story: 'God Is My Witness,' Part I," *McCall's*, April 1964, p. 125.

6. Billy Graham, "Are You Spending Your Life, or Investing It?" http//www.decisionmag.org.

7. Graham, "Billy Graham's Own Story," p. 122.

8. "Billy Graham: The Man at Home," p. 47.

9. William Martin, *A Prophet with Honor: The Billy Graham Story* (New York: William Morrow & Company, 1991), p. 61.

10. TV profile of Billy Graham, *Legends*, CNN, 1986.

11. William Martin, "Fifty Years: The Impact of Billy Graham's Ministry to the World," *Christianity Today*, November 13, 1995, p. 20.

12. Marshall Frady, *Billy Graham: A Parable of American Righteousness* (Boston: Little Brown & Company, 1979), p. 25.

13. Ibid., p. 28.

14. Ibid., p. 36.

15. Ibid., pp. 30–31.

16. Ibid.

17. Graham, "Billy Graham's Own Story, Part I," p. 124.

18. Stanley High, *Billy Graham* (New York: McGraw Hill, 1956), p. 103.

19. Frady, *Billy Graham*.

20. Stanley High, *Billy Graham* (New York: McGraw Hill, 1956), p. 107.

21. Frady, *Billy Graham*, p. 39.

22. Ibid., p. 40.

23. Biography.com, November 25, 1998, p. 6.

24. Ibid.

25. Graham, "Billy Graham's Own Story, Part I," p. 196.

26. Ibid., p. 197.

27. Julia Duin, "Congress Honors Graham: Graham Criticizes Clinton," *Insight*, June 3, 1996, p. 38.

28. Charles Hirshberg, "The Eternal Crusader," *Life*, November 1994, p. 108.

29. Graham, "Billy Graham's Own Story, Part I," p. 198.

30. Ibid.

31. Sue Ann Pressley, "At Bob Jones University, Gay Means 'Non Grata,'" *Washington Post*, November 4, 1998, p. A3.

32. Frady, *Billy Graham*, p. 96.

33. Billy Graham, "Billy Graham's Own Story, Part I," p. 200.

34. Ibid.

35. Ibid., p. 201.

36. Ibid.

37. Graham, "Are You Spending Your Life, or Investing It?"

38. Curtis Rist and Gail Cameron Wescott, "Spirit: The Long Road Home Slowed By Illness," *People*, November 14, 1996, p. 131.

39. Graham, "Billy Graham's Own Story, Part I," p. 201.

40. Ibid., p. 201.

41. Grady Wilson, *Count It All Joy* (Nashville: Broadman Press, 1984), p. 59.

42. Graham, "Billy Graham's Own Story, Part I," p. 202.

43. Ibid.

44. Billy Graham, "Billy Graham's Own Story: God is My Witness, Part II," *McCall's*, May 1964, p. 178.

45. Billy Graham, "Billy Graham's Own Story, Part I," p. 204.

46. Ruth Bell Graham, on her visit to China, 1988. From video provided by the Billy Graham Research Center, Wheaton, Illinois.

47. Billy Graham, "My Own Christmas Love Story," *Christian Herald*, November/December 1991, p. 19.

48. Patricia Daniels Cornwell, *A Time for Remembering: The Ruth Bell Graham Story* (San Francisco, Doubleday, 1983), p. 73.

49. Wendy Murray Zoba, "Billy's Rib," *Christianity Today*, November 13, 1995, p. 28.

50. Nancy Gibbs and Richard N. Ostling, "God's Billy Pulpit," *Time*, November 15, 1993, p. 75.

51. Graham, "My Own Christmas Love Story," p. 18.

52. "Billy Graham: The Man at Home," p. 44.

53. Cornwell, *A Time for Remembering*, pp. 73–74.

54. Billy Graham, *Just As I Am* (New York, HarperCollins Worldwide, 1997), p. 252.

55. *People Weekly*, February 12, 1996, p. 155.

56. Ibid.

57. Viviane Peter, "Rev. & Mrs. Billy Graham—How It Feels to Be a Crusader's Wife," *Parade*, March 8, 1970, p. 7.

58. Zoba, "Billy's Rib." *Christianity Today*, November 13, 1995, p. 28

59. Frady, *Billy Graham*, p. 357.

60. Graham, "Billy Graham's Own Story, Part I," p. 206.

61. Cornwell, *A Time for Remembering*, pp. 137–138.

62. Billy Graham, Little Rock, Arkansas, Crusade, January 30, 1990. From a video provided by the Billy Graham Research Center, Wheaton College, Illinois.

63. James Michael Beam, "I Can't Play God Any More," *McCall's*, January 1978, p. 100.

64. Hirshberg, "The Eternal Crusader," p. 107.

65. Frady, *Billy Graham*, p. 355.

66. "Billy Graham: The Man at Home," p. 44.

67. Frady, *Billy Graham*, p. 355.

68. John Pollock, "Dr. Bell Gave It to Me," *A Foreign Devil in China* (New York: World Wide Books, 1988), p. 238.

69. Frady, *Billy Graham*, p. 356.

70. Patricia Cornwell, *Ruth: A Portrait* (New York: Doubleday, 1997), p. 134.

71. Frady, *Billy Graham*, p. 281.

72. Mary Bishop, *Billy Graham: The Man and His Ministry* (New York, Grosset & Dunlop, 1978), p. 26.

73. Graham Training Center at The Cove, December 21, 1998.

74. Zoba, "Billy's Rib," p. 28.

75. Hirshberg, "The Eternal Crusader," p. 108.

76. "Billy Graham: The Man at Home," p. 45.

77. From Grace Films, The Canvas Cathedral, 1949. Film provided by the Billy Graham Research Center. Wheaton College, Illinois.

78. Ibid.

79. Billy Graham, "Prepare to Meet Thy God," *Revival in Our Time*, p. 124.

80. Graham, "Billy Graham's Own Story, Part II," p. 180.

81. Bishop, *Billy Graham*, p. 34.

82. Billy Graham, "What Ten Years Have Taught Me," *The Christian Century*, February 17, 1960, p. 186.

Billy Graham's Vision of Christianity

1. Billy Graham, "Billy Graham's Own Story: 'God Is My Witness,' Part II," *McCall's*, May 1964, p. 182.

2. Curtis Mitchell, *The Billy Graham London Crusade* (Minneapolis: World Wide Publications, 1966), pp. 15, 21, 33, 43.

3. Billy Graham, *Peace with God* (New York: Doubleday 1953), p. 38.

4. Ibid., p. 33.

5. Ibid., p. 36.

6. Martin, *A Prophet with Honor*, p. 156.

7. Nancy Gibbs and Richard N. Ostling, "God's Billy Pulpit," *Time*, November 15, 1993, p. 74.

8. Graham, *Peace with God*, pp. 38–39.

9. Ibid., p. 38.

10. Ibid., p. 41.

11. Ibid., p. 39.

12. Billy Graham, *Hour of Decision* (Television program, 1952), CN113, Film 188, Billy Graham Evangelistic Association.

13. Graham, *Peace with God*, p. 34.

14. Billy Graham, Denver, Colorado Crusade, February 5, 1988, from video provided by the Billy Graham Research Center, Wheaton College, Illinois.

15. Billy Graham, "The Only Way," Billy Graham's message, August 1998, *Decision on Line*. From Billy Graham, *A Biblical Standard for Evangelists* (Minneapolis: Billy Graham Evangelistic Association, World Wide Publications).

16. Edward B. Fiske, "The Closest Thing to a White House Chaplain," *The New York Times Magazine*, June 8, 1969, p. 109.

17. Billy Graham, 1988 visit to China, from a video provided by the Billy Graham Research Center, Wheaton, Illinois.

18. Graham, "The Only Way."

19. Billy Graham, *Just As I Am* (New York: HarperCollins Worldwide, 1997), p. 355.

20. Graham, "The Only Way."

21. Graham, *Peace with God*, p. 24.

22. Billy Graham, *World Aflame* (New York: Doubleday, 1965), p. 99.

23. John Pollock, *To All the Nations: The Billy Graham Story* (San Francisco: Harper & Row, 1985), p. 40.

24. Billy Graham, "Billy Graham's Own Story, God is My Witness, Part II," *McCall's*, May 1964, p. 179.

25. David W. Cloud, "Billy Graham's Disobedience to the Word of God," http://wayoflife.org/~dcloud/, October 6, 1995.

26. *Time*, July 24, 1972.

27. *Charisma*, March 1991, p. 98.

28. Cloud, "Billy Graham's Disobedience."

29. Billy Graham, *Hope for the Troubled Heart* (Minneapolis: Grason, 1991), p. 157.

30. "Candid Conversation with the Evangelist," *Christianity Today*, July 17, 1981, p. 23.

31. Graham, p. 151.

32. Ibid.

33. Ibid., p. 158.

34. "Billy Graham: The Man at Home," *The Saturday Evening Post*, Spring 1972, p. 106.

35. Billy Graham, Angels: *God's Secret Agents* (New York: Doubleday & Company, 1975), p. 18.

36. Ibid., p. 30

37. Billy Graham, *Facing Death and the Life After* (Waco, Tex.: Word Books, 1987), p. 211.

38. *Boston Post*, January 16, 1950.

39. Ibid.

40. Fiske, "The Closest Thing to a White House Chaplain."

41. *The David Frost Show*, Westinghouse Broadcasting, 1969. David Frost, *Billy Graham: Personal Thoughts of a Public Man* (Colorado Springs: Chariot Victor Publishing, Cook Communications, 1997), p. 169.

42. Nancy Gibbs and Richard N. Ostling, "God's Billy Pulpit," *Time*, November 15, 1993, p. 70.

43. Graham, *Hope for the Troubled Heart*, p. 217.

44. Graham, *World Aflame*, p. 255.

45. Ibid., p. 259.

46. Graham, *Facing Death and the Life After*, p. 235.

47. Ibid., p. 222.

48. *USA Today*, April 16, 1992 cited at Bible Discernment Ministries, revised January 1994, Internet. www.rapidnet.com/~jbeard/bdm/exposes/graham/general.ht

49. "Come on Down for Jesus," *New Statesman and Society*, June 23, 1989, p. 25.

50. Curtis Rist and Gail Cameron Wescott, "Spirit: The Long Road Home Slowed by Illness," *People*, November 14, 1996, p. 131.

51. Billy Graham, *Angels: God's Secret Agents* (New York: Doubleday 1975), p. 64.

205

52. Billy Graham, *The Holy Spirit* (New York: International Press, 1988), p. 454.

53. Frady, *Billy Graham*.

54. Billy Graham, *Approaching Hoofbeats: The Four Horsemen of the Apocalypse* (Minneapolis: Grason, 1983), p. 86.

55. Graham, *Just As I Am*, p. 70.

56. Billy Graham, "My Answer," *The Christian Herald and Signs of Our Times*, April 22, 1961.

57. "God's Billy Pulpit," *Time*, www.rapidnet.com/njbeard/bdm/exposes/graham/general.ht November 15, 1993. Bible Discernment Ministries, revised January 1994, Internet.

58. Graham, *Facing Death and the Life After*, p. 220.

59. Graham, *Asheville Citizen*, March 2, 1960.

60. Graham, *Peace with God*, p. 49.

61. "Candid Conversation with the Evangelist," p. 21.

62. *The David Frost Show*, Westinghouse Broadcasting, 1970.

63. Billy Graham, *The Billy Graham Christian Workers Handbook* (Minneapolis: World Wide Publications, 1984). Frost, *Billy Graham*, p. 114.

64. David Aikman, "Preachers, Politics and Temptation," *Time*, May 28, 1990, p. 13.

65. "The Reverend Billy Graham Talking with David Frost," PBS, January 23, 1993.

66. "Reverend Billy Graham Talking with David Frost," p. 115.

67. Billy Graham, "Road Rules for Life," http://www.decisionmag.org.

68. Billy Graham, *My Answer* (World's Work), excerpted from the book by the *Liverpool Echo*, Liverpool, Lancashire, England, April 27, 1991.

69. The David Frost Show, 1969. Frost, *Billy Graham*.

70. Garth M. Rosell,"Grace Under Fire," *Christianity Today*, November 13, 1995, p. 33.

71. Graham, *Just As I Am*, p. 683.

72. Graham, *Peace with God*, p. 81.

73. Graham, *Angels*, p. 150.

74. Ibid., p. 152.

75. Graham, *Facing Death and the Life After*, p. 39.

76. Hirshberg,"The Eternal Crusader."

77. "Billy Graham: The Man at Home," p. 106.

78. Graham, *Facing Death and the Life After*, p. 47.

79. Ibid., p. 141.

80. "Frost on Sunday: Interview with Billy Graham," TV-AM, Great Britain, 1989. Frost, *Billy Graham*, p. 156.

81. Frady, *Billy Graham*, p. 397.

82. Graham, *World Aflame*, pp. 1–2.

83. Frady, *Billy Graham*.

84. Billy Graham, "At Times a Sword and Fire," *Christianity Today*, December 17, 1982, p. 23.

85. Billy Graham, *Storm Warning* (Dallas: Word Publishing, 1992), pp. 23–24.

86. Ibid., p. 24.

87. Graham, *Peace with God*, pp. 40–41.

88. Graham, *Storm Warning*, p. 270.

89. Graham, *World Aflame*, p. xvi.

90. Kathy Lynn Grossman, "Withholding Judgment Billy Graham Humble Before God, Clinton, USA." *USA Today*, February 5, 1998.

91. "Candid Conversation with the Evangelist," p. 22.

92. Hirshberg, "The Eternal Crusader," p. 116.

93. Grossman,"Withholding Judgment Billy Graham Humble Before God, Clinton, USA."

94. Fiske, "The Closest Thing to a White House Chaplain," p. 116.

95. "Billy Graham: The Man at Home," p. 45.

Billy Graham's Work

1. Billy Graham, "What Ten Years Have Taught Me," *The Christian Century*, February 17, 1960, p. 187.

2. Billy Graham, *The Holy Spirit* (New York: International Press, 1988), p. 454.

3. Ibid.

4. Graham, "What Ten Years Have Taught Me," p. 186.

5. Ibid.

6. Poster at the Billy Graham Training Center at The Cove, Asheville, North Carolina, December 21, 1998.

7. Mary Bishop, *Billy Graham: The Man and His Ministry* (New York, Grosset & Dunlop, 1978), p. 32.

8. Harold L. Myra, "William Franklin Graham: Seventy Exceptional Years," *Christianity Today*, November 18, 1988, p. 20.

9. Beam, "I Can't Play God Anymore," p. 158.

10. John Pollock, *Billy Graham: The Authorized Biography* (New York: McGraw-Hill, 1966), p. 215.

11. Graham, *The Holy Spirit*, p. 454.

12. Ibid., p. 455.

13. Edward B. Fiske, "The Closest Thing to a White House Chaplain," *The New York Times Magazine*, June 8, 1969, p. 116.

14. Brunham, *Billy Graham: A Mission Accomplished*, p. 133.

15. Carl F. H. Henry, "Firm on the Fundamentals," *Christianity Today*, November 18, 1988, p. 19.

16. Bishop, *Billy Graham*, p. 16.

17. Billy Graham, "Whatever God Asks," taken from *A Biblical Standard for Evangelists* and published on http://www.decisionmag.org.

18. Myra, "William Franklin Graham," p. 19.

19. Richard N. Ostling, "Religion: Summons to the 'Unknowns,' Billy Graham Organizes a Massive Training School for Evangelists," *Time*, July 28, 1986, p. 69.

20. Garth M. Rosell, "Grace Under Fire," *Christianity Today*, November 13, 1995, p. 34.

21. Nancy Gibbs and Richard N. Ostling, "God's Billy Pulpit," *Time*, November 15, 1993, p. 70.

22. *London Evening News*, February 23, 1954.

23. Hannen Swaffer, *London Daily Herald*, February 20, 1954.

24. Billy Graham, *Just As I Am* (New York: HarperCollins Worldwide, 1997), p. 216.

25. Ibid., p. 184.

26. Frank Colquhoun, *The Harringay Story: The Official Story of the Billy Graham Greater London Crusade, 1954* (London: Hodder & Stoughton, 1955), p. 18.

27. "The Crusade for Britain," *Time*, March 8, 1954, p. 72.

28. Billy Graham, "Billy Graham's Own Story, God Is My Witness, Part II," *McCall's*, May 1964, p. 183.

29. Ibid., p. 184.

30. Bishop, *Billy Graham*, p. 69.

31. Martin, *A Prophet with Honor*, p. 181.

32. Billy Graham, "Billy Graham's Own Story, God Is My Witness, Part I," *McCall's*, April 1964, p. 122.

33. Billy Graham, *Just As I Am*, p. 226.

34. "Billy's Conquest," *Newsweek*, July 12, 1954 , p. 68.

35. Graham, *Just As I Am*, p. 250.

36. The New York Crusade, 1957, film provided by the Billy Graham Research Center, Wheaton College, Wheaton, Illinois.

37. Graham, "What Ten Years Have Taught Me," p. 187.

38. Philip Tracy, "Billy Graham Plays the Garden," *Commonweal*, July 25, 1969, pp. 457–458.

39. John Pollock, *To All the Nations: The Billy Graham Story* (San Francisco: Harper & Row, 1985), p. 107.

40 "Billy Graham, The Man at Home," *Saturday Evening Post*, Spring 1972, p. 43.

41. Edward E. Plowman, "Billy Graham: The Gospel Truth in Moscow," *The Saturday Evening Post* , September 1982, p. 68.

42. Ibid., p. 69.

43. Graham, *Just As I Am*, p. 502.

44. Patricia Cornwell, *Ruth—A Portrait* (New York: Doubleday, 1997), p. 165.

45. Gerald Strober, *Billy Graham: His Life and His Faith* (Waco, Tex.: Word Books, 1977), pp. 126–127.

46. Margaret Shannon, "Where Billy Graham's Sawdust Trail Begins," *The Atlanta Constitution and Journal Magazine*, January 25, 1970, p. 9.

47. Martin E. Marty, "Reflections on Graham by a Former Grump," *Christianity Today*, November 18, 1988, p. 25.

48. Jan Jarboe Russell, "Billy Graham's Daughter Keeps the Faith," *Good Housekeeping*, January 1997, p. 14.

49. Charles W. Dullea, S. J., *A Catholic Looks at Billy Graham* (New York: Paulist Press, 1973), pp. 37–38.

50. Joan Rattner Heilman, "Billy Graham's Daughter Answers His Critics," *Good Housekeeping*, June 1973, p. 157.

51. "Reverend Billy Graham Talking with David Frost," PBS, January 23, 1993.

52. Myra, "William Franklin Graham," p. 226.

53. Billy Graham, *Just As I Am*, p. 185.

54. Myra, "William Franklin Graham," p. 21.

55. Simpson, *Charlotte News*, January 28, 1970.

56. Gary and Polly Paddock, *Charlotte Observer*, June 30, 1973.

57. Pollock, *Billy Graham*, p. 89.

58. T. W. Wilson, "Without Shades of Gray," *Christianity Today*, November 13, 1995, p. 33.

59. Richard N. Ostling, "And Then There Was Billy At 70, The Century's Most Popular Protestant Is Busier Than Ever," *Time*, November 14, 1988, p. 86.

60. "Candid Conversation with the Evangelist," *Christianity Today*, July 17, 1981, p. 20.

61. "Doubts and Certainties: David Frost interview with Billy Graham," BBC-2, 1964.

62. Wendy Murray Zoba, "Billy's Rib," *Christianity Today*, November 13, 1995, p. 28.

63. *Good Morning America* with David Hartman, September 23, 1977, from video provided by the Billy Graham Research Center, Wheaton College, Illinois.

64. Frady, *Billy Graham*, pp. 283–284.

65. Beam, "I Can't Play God Anymore," p. 156.

66. *The David Frost Show*, Westinghouse Broadcasting, 1970.

67. Tamara Henry, "Billy Graham: Just as He Is," *USA Today*, May 15, 1997, p. 8D.

68. Ibid.

69. Charles W. Dullea, S. J., *A Catholic Looks at Billy Graham* (New York: Paulist Press, 1973), p. 50.

70. Myra, "William Franklin Graham," p. 17.

71. "In the Beginning: Billy Graham Recounts the Origins of *Christianity Today*," *Christianity Today*, July 17, 1981, p. 26.

72. Billy Graham, "Steps to Peace with God" and "Commitment to Jesus Christ," *The Way*, Billy Graham Evangelistic Association, 1998.

Billy Graham and Earthly Issues

1. Charles Hirshberg, "The Eternal Crusader," *Life*, November 1994, p. 116.

2. Billy Graham, "Time Shortage," http://www.aliveonline.org.

3. Ibid.

4. Billy Graham, "Road Rules for Life," http://www.decisionmag.org.

5. Billy Graham, *Hope for the Troubled Heart* (Minneapolis: Grayson, 1991), p. 105.

6. Ibid., p.187

7. Billy Graham, "At Times a Sword and Fire," *Christianity Today*, December 17, 1982, p. 23.

8. Billy Graham, *The Secret of Happiness* (Garden City, N.Y.: Doubleday & Co., 1955), published on http://www.decsionmag.org.

9. Billy Graham, "Real Thanksgiving," *Christian Herald*, November/December 1989, p. 13.

10. Billy Graham, *Hope for the Troubled Heart*, p. 115.

11. Graham, *The Secret of Happiness*.

12. Billy Graham, "Billy Graham's Own Story: 'God Is My Witness,' Part I,' *McCall's*, April 1964, p. 204.

13. Billy Graham, "Billy Graham's Own Story: 'God Is My Witness' Part II," *McCall's*, May 1964, p. 119.

14. "Candid Conversation with the Evangelist," *Christianity Today*, July 17, 1981, p. 23.

15. Mary Bishop, *Billy Graham: The Man and His Ministry* (New York: Grosset & Dunlop, 1978), p. 13.

16. Jan Jarobe Russell, "Billy Graham's Daughter Keeps the Faith," *Good Housekeeping*, January, 1997, p. 24.

17. Billy Graham, Billy Graham Evangelistic Association, October 18, 1998, www.billygraham.org/newscommentary2.asp.

18. Harold L. Myra, "William Franklin Graham: Seventy Exceptional Years," *Christianity Today*, November 18, 1988, p. 23.

19. Nancy Gibbs and Richard N. Ostling, "God's Billy Pulpit," *Time*, November 15, 1993, p. 75.

20. Bishop, *Billy Graham*, p. 74.

21. "William Franklin Graham: Seventy Exceptional Years," *Christianity Today*, November 18, 1988, p.23

22. Ibid.

23. William Martin, *A Prophet with Honor: The Billy Graham Story* (New York: William Morrow & Company, 1991) p. 257.

24. *Charlotte News*, July 3, 1959.

25. Billy Graham quote, Denver, Colorado Crusade, February 5, 1988, from video provided by the Billy Graham Research Center, Wheaton College, Illinois.

26. *Bloomington Herald-Times*, October 10, 1993 [Bible Discernment Ministries, revised January 1994, Internet] www.rapidnet.com/~jbeard/bdm/exposes/Graham/general.ht

27. *Cleveland Plain Dealer* [Bible Discernment Ministries, revised 1994, Internet]

28. P.R.R., "Billy Graham on TV, Religion, and More," *TV Guide*, August 6, 1994, p. 20.

29. "A Graham Follow-up," *The Christian Century*, April 11, 1973, pp. 414–415.

30. The *Larry King Show*, "Life After 50," *CNN Interactive*, October 26, 1998.

31. Graham, *Hope for the Troubled Heart*, p. 186.

32. Ibid., p. 184.

33. Billy Graham, *My Answer*, excerpted from *World's Work* by *The Liverpool Echo*, Liverpool, Lancashire, England, April 27, 1961.

34. David Meeks, Gannett News Service, September 14, 1998, available at Electric Library.

35. Billy Graham, "Letting God Shape Us," http://www.decisionmag.org.

36. P.R.R., "Billy Graham on TV, Religion, and More."

37. Graham, "At Times a Sword and Fire."

38. Billy Graham, "Billy Graham: The Man at Home," *Saturday Evening Post*, Spring 1972, p. 47.

39. Billy Graham, *My Answer*.

40. Joan Rattner Heilman, "Graham's Daughter Answers His Critics," *Good Housekeeping*, June 1973, p. 153.

41. Bishop, *Billy Graham*, p. 12.

42. Ibid.

43. Betty Frist, *My Neighbors, the Billy Grahams* (Nashville, Tenn: Broadman Press, 1983), p. 103.

44. Heilman, "Graham's Daughter Answers His Critics," pp. 156–157.

45. Frist, *My Neighbors*, p. 115.

46. Franklin Graham, *Rebel with a Cause: Finally Comfortable Being Graham* (Nashville, Thomas Nelson, Inc., 1995), pp. 16–17.

47. Ibid., p. 20.

48. Ibid., pp. 26–27.

49. Frist, *My Neighbors*, p. 39.

50. Jeffrey L. Sheler, "After the Legend," *U.S. News & World Report*, May 3, 1993, p. 71.

51. http://www.freep.com/news/religion/qgrams24.htm

52. Dan Wooding, "Billy Graham: Reaching 2.5 Billion People," *Saturday Evening Post*, March 13, 1996, p. 42.

53. David Van Biema, "Religion: In the name of the Father," *Time*, May 13, 1996, p. 66.

54. Patricia Cornwell, *Ruth—A Portrait: The Ruth Bell Graham Story* (New York: Doubleday, 1997), p. 167.

55. Gigi Graham Tchividjian, *Passing It On* (New York: McCracken Press, 1993), p. 26.

56. Billy Graham, *World Aflame* (New York: Doubleday 1965), p. 3.

57. "Billy Graham: The Man at Home," *Saturday Evening Post* (Spring 1972), p. 105.

58. Billy Graham, *Storm Warning* (Dallas: Word Publishing, 1992), pp. 233–234.

59. Julia Duin, "Congress Honors Graham: Graham Criticizes Clinton," *Insight*, June 3, 1996, p. 38.

60. Gibbs and Ostling, "God's Billy Pulpit," p. 70.

61. The *Larry King Show*, "Life After 50."

62. Billy Graham, *Facing Death and the Life After* (Waco, Texas: Word Books, 1987), p. 121.

63. Graham, "Letting God Shape Us."

64. Graham, *World Aflame*, p. 13.

65. Cathy Lynn Grossman, "Withholding Judgment Billy Graham Humble Before God, Clinton, USA." *USA Today*, February 5, 1998, available at Electric Library.

66. Billy Graham, "You Can Know the Truth," http://www.decision mag.org.

67. Marshall Frady, *Billy Graham: A Parable of American Righteousness* (Boston: Little, Brown & Company, 1979), p. 68.

68. "Billy Graham on Race," *Journal of Blacks in Higher Education*, available at Ethnic News Watch, on the Internet, September 30, 1996.

69. Ibid.

70. John Pollock, *To All the Nations: The Billy Graham Story* (San Francisco: Harper & Row, 1985), p. 104.

71. Ibid.

72. Edward Gilbreath, "Billy Graham Had a Dream," *Christianity Today*, January 12, 1998, p. 44 .

73. Pollock, *To All the Nations*, p. 105.

74. Billy Graham, "No Solution to Race Problem: 'At the Point of Bayonets,'" *U.S. News & World Report*, April 25, 1960, p. 94 .

75. Bishop, *Billy Graham*, p. 84.

76. William Martin, *A Prophet With Honor: The Billy Graham Story* (New York: William Morrow & Company, 1991), p. 247.

77. Martin, *A Prophet with Honor*, p. 250.

78. Billy Graham, *Just As I Am* (New York: HarperCollins Worldwide, 1997), p. 351.

79. Billy Graham, "Racism and the Evangelical Church," *Christianity Today*, October 4, 1993, p. 27.

80. Billy Graham, "My Answer," *The Christian Herald and Signs of Our Times*, April 15, 1961.

81. Graham, "Billy Graham Makes Plea for an End to Intolerance," p. 143.

82. Billy Graham, "No Solution to Race Problem," p. 94 .

83. Ibid.

84. Graham, "Billy Graham Makes Plea for an End to Intolerance," p. 140.

85. Graham, "No Solution to Race Problem," pp. 94–95.

86. Charles Hirshberg, "The Eternal Crusader," *Life*, November 1994, p. 111.

87. Graham, "Billy Graham Makes Plea for an End to Intolerance," p. 146.

88. Pollock, *To All the Nations*, p. 106.

89. Graham, "Billy Graham Makes Plea for an End to Intolerance," p. 144.

90. Ibid., p. 151.

91. Bible Discernment Ministries, revised January 1994. www.rapid net.com/njbeard/bdm/exposes/graham/general.ht.

92. Billy Graham, "What Ten Years Have Taught Me," *The Christian Century*, February 17, 1960, p. 188.

93. James Michael Beam, "I Can't Play God Anymore," *McCall's*, January, 1978, p. 158.

94. William Martin, "Fifty Years With Billy," *Christianity Today*, November 13, 1995, p. 22.

95. Ibid., p. 23.

96. *Philadelphia Evening Bulletin*, May 24, 1966, Bible Discernment Ministries, revised January 1994. www.rapidnet.com/~jbeard/bdm/exposes/graham/general.ht.

97. Graham, *Just As I Am*, p. 390.

98. Paul Smith, "Belmont Abbey Confers Honorary Degree," The Gastonia Gazette, November 22, 1967; David W. Cloud, "Billy Graham's Disobedience to the Word of God," October 6, 1995. http://wayoflife.org/~dcloud/.

99. Ibid.

100. *Minneapolis Star*, April 22, 1972, Bible Discernment Ministries, revised January 1994. www.rapidnet.com/njbeard/bdm/exposes/graham/general.ht.

101. *The Gospel Standard*, February 1986, Bible Discernment Ministries, revised 1994. www.rapidnet.com/njbeard/bdm/exposes/graham/general.ht.

102. Graham, *Just As I Am*, p. 354.

103. Beam, "I Can't Play God Anymore," p. 158.

104. Billy Graham, "Graham's View from Japan," *Christianity Today*, February 7, 1994, p. 55.

105. Ibid.

106. Bible Discernment Ministries, revised January 1994. www.rapidnet.com/njbeard/bdm/exposes/graham/general.ht.

107. "Candid Conversation with the Evangelist," p. 20

108. Ibid., p. 19.

109. "Billy Graham: The Man at Home," *The Saturday Evening Post*, Spring 1972, p. 105.

110. *Michigan City News-Dispatch*, June 8, 1963 Bible Discernment Ministries, revised January 1994. www.rapidnet.com/njbeard/bdm/exposes/graham/general.ht.

111. *Saturday Evening Post*, January/February 1980, Bible Discernment Ministries, revised January 1994. www.rapidnet.com/njbeard/bdm/exposes/graham/general.ht.

112. Religious News Service Dispatch, *New Neutralism II*, September 27, 1979, p.40, Bible Discernment Ministries, revised January 1994. www.rapidnet.com/njbeard/bdm/exposes/graham/general.ht.

113. *Christianity Today*, July 17, 1981, Bible Discernment Ministries, revised January 1994. www.rapidnet.com/njbeard/bdm/exposes/graham/general.ht.

114. "Candid Conversation with the Evangelist," p. 21.

115. *Phil Donahue Show*, October 11, 1979, Bible Discernment Ministries, revised January 1994. www.rapidnet.com/njbeard/bdm/exposes/graham/general.ht.

116. *Foundation*, Vol. 5, no. 5, 1984, Bible Discernment Ministries, revised 1994. www.rapidnet.com/njbeard/bdm/exposes/graham/general.ht.

117. *Today*, June 8, 1989, Bible Discernment Ministries, revised 1994. www.rapidnet.com/njbeard/bdm/exposes/graham/general.ht.

118. Graham, *Just As I Am*, pp. 428, 429.

119. J. D. Douglas, "He Put It Over with Love," *Christianity Today*, July 7, 1972, p. 4 .

120. Ian Paisley, "Billy Graham's Tragic Romeward Run, "*O Timothy* magazine, Vol. 10, no. 9 (1993).

121. Ibid.

Graham's Life in Politics

1. Robert Sherrill, "Preachers to Power," *MacLeans,* July 1998, p. 14.

2. Cathy Lynn Grossman, *USA Today*, February 5, 1998, available at Electric Library.

3. Billy Graham, "Graham's View from Japan," *Christianity Today*, February 7, 1994, p. 55.

4. Billy Graham, *Storm Warning* (Dallas: Word Publishing, 1992), p. 71.

5. "The Whisky Rebellion," *Time*, February, 28, 1949, p. 18.

6. *Boston Record*, January 11, 1950.

7. Jay Walker, *Billy Graham: A Life in Word and Deed* (New York: Avon Books, 1998), p. 142.

8. Lynn Henzerling, "Attendance Falls After Papers Hit Graham's Reticence on Bomb," *Asheville Citizen*, January 26, 1960.

9. Nancy Gibbs and Richard C. Ostling, "God's Billy Pulpit," *Time*, November 15, 1993, p. 70.

10. "Billy Graham: The Man at Home," *The Saturday Evening Post*, Spring 1972, p. 105.

11. Joan Rattner Heilman, "Billy Graham's Daughter Answers His Critics," *Good Housekeeping*, June 1973, p. 82.

12. Martin, *A Prophet with Honor,* p. 300.

13. "Billy Graham: "The Man at Home," p. 105.

14. Gibbs and Ostling, "God's Billy Pulpit," p. 70.

15. Neyland Stadium Crusade, Knoxville, Tennessee, 1970, film provided by the Billy Graham Research Center, Wheaton College, Illinois.

16. Billy Graham, *Just As I Am* (New York: HarperCollins Worldwide, 1997), p. 382.

17. Robert Sherrill, "Preachers to Power," *The Nation*, July 13, 1998, p. 13.

18. Graham, *Just As I Am*, p. 381.

19. Ibid.

20. Martin, *A Prophet with Honor*, p. 146.

21. Sherrill, "Preachers to Power," *The Nation*, p. 14.

22. "Graham Denounces Dissenters," *The Christian Century*, May 17, 1967, p. 645.

23. "Come on Down for Jesus," *New Statesman and Society*, June 23, 1989, p. 25.

24. "Quote of the Week," *New Republic*, January 6–13, 1973, p.11.

25. Billy Graham, Billy Graham Evangelistic Association, cited at www. billygraham.org/newscommentary2.asp, October 18, 1998.

26. Merle Miller, *Plain Speaking* (New York: Berkeley, 1973), p. 363.

27. William G. Mclaughlin, Billy Graham, *Revivalist in a Secular Age* (New York: Ronald Press, 1960), pp. 243–244.

28. Ibid., p. 147.

29. "Billy Graham: The Man at Home," p. 44.

30. Graham, *Just As I Am*, p. 389.

31. Ibid., pp. 398–399.

32. Ibid., p. 400.

33. "Billy Graham: the Man at Home," *Saturday Evening Post*, Spring 1972, p. 105.

34. Edward B. Fiske, "The Closest Thing to a White House Chaplain," *The New York Times Magazine*, June 8, 1969.

35. Graham, *Just As I Am*, p. 403.

36. Patricia Daniels Cornwell, *A Time for Remembering: The Ruth Bell Graham Story* (San Francisco: Harper & Row, 1983), p.195.

37. Martin, *A Prophet with Honor*, p. 349.

38. Graham, *Just As I Am*, pp. 403–404.

39. Ibid.

40. Ibid., p. 391.

41. Charles Hirshberg, "The Eternal Crusader," *Life*, November 1994, p. 111.

42. Frady, *Billy Graham*, p. 16.

43. "Come on Down for Jesus," p. 25.

44. Frady, *Billy Graham*, p. 479.

45. Hirshberg, "The Eternal Crusader," p. 110.

46. Mary Bishop Lacy, *Charlotte Observer*, December 31, 1975

47. Martha Rainy, *Charlotte News*, August 9, 1974

48. David Aikman, "Preachers, Politics and Temptation," *Time*, May 28, 1990, p. 12.

49. Graham, *Just As I Am*, p. 468.

50. Ibid., p. 471.

51. Martin, *A Prophet With Honor*, p. 463.

52. Ibid.

53. Graham, *Just As I Am*, p. 533.

54. Ibid., pp. 536–537.

55. Ibid., pp. 585–585.

56. David Meeks, Gannett News Service, September 14, 1998, available at Electric Library.

57 Ibid.

58. Sherrill, "Preachers to Power," p. 12.

59. Ibid.

60. Allan Fotheringham, "A Land of Assassins and Glorious Sunsets," *MacLeans*, April 3, 1995, p. 68.

61. President Bill Clinton, remarks at a dinner honoring Billy and Ruth Graham (Transcript), Vol. 32, Weekly Compilation of Presidential Documents, May 6, 1996, p. 784.

62. Graham, *Just As I Am*, p. 235.

63. John Pollock, *To All the Nations: The Billy Graham Story* (San Francisco: Harper & Row, 1985), p. 69.

64. Billy Graham, *World Aflame* (New York: Doubleday, 1965), p. 1.

65. Graham, *Just As I Am*, p. 297.

66. "Kim Il Sung, Up Close and Personal," *New Yorker*, March 14, 1994.

67. John Pollock, *Billy Graham: The Authorized Biography* (New York: McGraw-Hill, 1966), p. 153.

68. Harold L. Myra,, "William Franklin Graham: Seventy Exceptional Years," *Christianity Today*, November 18, 1988, p. 19.

69. On a poster at The Billy Graham Training Center, Asheville, North Carolina, December 21, 1998.

The Critics

1. Marshall Frady, *Billy Graham: A Parable of American Righteousness*, (Boston: Little, Brown & Company, 1979), p. 493.

2. Nancy Gibbs and Richard N. Ostling, "God's Billy Pulpit," *Time*, November 15, 1993, p. 72.

3. Martin E. Marty, "Billy Graham Made His Own Mark, But He Said It Was In God's Hand," *Star Tribune*, May 10, 1997, p. 05B.

4. Gibbs and Ostling, "God's Billy Pulpit," p. 70.

5. Ibid., p. 73.

6. Billy Graham, "My Answer," *The Christian Herald and Signs of Our Times*, April 22, 1961.

7. William Martin, "Fifty Years With Billy," *Christianity Today*, November 13, 1995, p. 20.

8. Joan Lunden, ABC's *Good Morning America*, July 12, 1993, Bible Discernment Ministries, revised January 1994. www.rapidnet.com/~jbeard/bdm/exposes/graham/general.ht

9. Billy Graham, "God's View of Tolerance," http://www.decision mag.org.

10. Ibid.

11.John Pollock, *Billy Graham: The Authorized Biography* (New York, McGraw-Hill Book Company, 1966), p. 91.

12. Reinhold Niebuhr, "Proposal to Billy Graham," *The Christian Century*, August 8, 1956, p. 922.

13. Ibid., p. 921.

14. Reinhold Niebuhr, "Literalism, Individualism and Billy Graham," *The Christian Century*, May 23, 1956, p. 642.

15. Pollock, *Billy Graham*, p. 221.

16. Dr. Brian Welbeck, *Reynold's News*, May 22, 1955.

17. Carl F. H. Henry, "Firm on the Fundamentals" *Christianity Today*, November 18, 1988, p. l9.

18. Associated Press, "African Witch Doctors Picket Meetings Preceding Graham's Crusade in Kisumu, *Asheville Times*, February 29, 1960, p. 6.

Looking Back on a Long Life

1. Billy Graham, Denver, Colorado Crusade, February 5, 1988, from a video provided by the Billy Graham Research Center, Wheaton College, Illinois.

2. "Candid Conversation with the Evangelist," *Christianity Today*, July 17, 1981, p. 18.

3. James Michael Beam, "I Can't Play God Anymore," *McCall's*, January 1978, p. 156.

4. Ibid., p. 158.

5. Billy Graham, "What Ten Years Have Taught Me," *The Christian Century*, February 17, 1960, p. 186.

6. Beam, "I Can't Play God Anymore," p. 156.

7. Billy Graham, *Approaching Hoofbeats: The Four Horsemen of the Apocalypse* (Waco, Tex.: World Books, 1983), p. 91.

8. Billy Graham, "Billy Graham's Own Story, God Is My Witness, Part I," *McCall's*, April 1964, p. 122.

9. Billy Graham, "Whatever God Asks," *Decision Magazine*, January 1999.

10. The *Larry King Show*, "Life After 50." CNN Interactive, October 26, 1998.

11. Jay Walker, *Billy Graham: A Life in Word and Deed* (New York: Avon Books, 1998), p. 171.

12. "Life After 50."

13. Franklin Graham, video of Little Rock, Arkansas crusade, January 30, 1990. Video provided by the Billy Graham Research Center, Wheaton College, Illinois.

14. Paul Smith, "Belmont Abbey Confers Honorary Degree," *The Gastonia Gazette*, November 22, 1967; David W. Cloud, "Billy Graham's Disobedience to the Word of God," October 6, 1995, http://wayoflife.org /~dcloud.

15. Cathy Lynn Grossman, "Withholding Judgment: Billy Graham Humble Before God, Clinton, USA." *USA Today*, February 5, 1998, available at Electric Library.

16. Ibid.

17. Charles Hirshberg, "The Eternal Crusader" *Life*, November 1994, p. 116.

18. "Reverend Billy Graham talking with David Frost," PBS, January 29, 1993. David Frost, *Billy Graham: Personal Thoughts of a Public Man*, (Colorado Springs: Chariot Victor Publishing, Cook Communications, 1997), p. 173.